D0927166

ON INTERPRETATION

ON INTERPRETATION

Sociology for Interpreters of Natural and Cultural History

Edited by
Gary E. Machlis
Donald R. Field

OREGON STATE UNIVERSITY PRESS
Corvallis, Oregon

The paper in this book meets the guidelines for permanence and durability of the Committee on Production Guidelines for Book Longevity of the Council on Library Resources.

Cover etching by Sally Graves Machlis.

Library of Congress Cataloging in Publication Data
Main entry under title:

On Interpretation.

Includes bibliographical references and index.
1. Tour guides (Persons)—Addresses, essays, lectures. 2. Recreation areas—Interpretive programs—Addresses, essays, lectures. 3. Recreation—Social aspects—Addresses, essays, lectures. I. Machlis, Gary E. II. Field, Donald R.

| G154.7.05 | 1984 | 306'.48 | 83-22017 |

ISBN O-87071-339-6

FOREWORD

Interpreting natural and cultural history has always been a hallmark of the National Park Service. The importance of interpretation to the mission of the agency has been demonstrated through the years, and the cadre of professionals who perform these services today is an essential arm of park management. More recently, sociology was added to the NPS science program in 1968. Our basic goals for the sociology program are to better understand the people who visit parks and to infuse this knowledge into various facets of park management.

So it is quite appropriate that Drs. Machlis and Field have prepared a volume that applies sociology to interpretation. They point to a new and growing partnership between sociologist and interpreter and call for expanding this partnership beyond the National Park Service to the many public and private organizations that interpret natural and cultural history. This is crucial, because the challenges of a dynamic future will surely place greater demands on professional interpreters. Increased knowledge about people and human behavior and additional training in the social sciences will enhance interpreters' ability to meet those demands.

The editors of this important volume have learned this first-hand through their ongoing research on people in parks and their work with National Park Service Cooperative Park Studies Units in the Pacific Northwest. Their experience in applied sociology adds credence to what they say.

On Interpretation is especially useful because it brings together a rich set of sociological ideas for practicing interpreters to consider. I also urge students training to become interpreters to consider the ideas presented. Whether we work for a local historical society, state forestry department, or federal agency, we are all servants of the public. The better we communicate with the public, the better we serve the agencies we represent.

RUSSELL E. DICKENSON, *Director*
National Park Service
U.S. Department of Interior

PREFACE

The sociological study of leisure behavior has a comparatively long history, originating in the United States soon after World War II. Yet it was not until the 1960s and 1970s, when sociologists and other behavioral scientists joined resource-related academic programs (such as schools of forestry), that the study of human behavior in outdoor leisure settings began to flourish. Added impetus was provided by the development of social science research programs in public agencies like the U.S. Forest Service and the National Park Service.

Within these emerging university and agency research programs, attention has often been directed at specific relationships between people and recreational resources. Examples range from human impact on the back country to littering in developed campgrounds. This book focuses on one such set of relationships between people and resources.

The theme of *On Interpretation* is the application of sociology to interpretation; however, this book is not a complete treatise on the subject. We do not, for example, discuss research that evaluates public response to interpretive programs, nor do we address research on the comparative effectiveness of various media. Rather, this collection examines selected clientele groups for whom interpreters provide natural and cultural history programs. It is directed toward the advanced interpreter, one who has experience in public contacts and interpretive techniques.

It is the advanced interpreter who now is responsible for planning creative and cost-effective programs that respond to the needs of contemporary visitors, the demands of resource protection, and management constraints. These men and women, together with agency administrators, graduate students, and other social scientists interested in outdoor leisure settings, are *On Interpretation's* intended audience.

Visitors to public parks, forests, and urban facilities such as zoos and aquariums are a diverse lot. It is a premise of this book that as interpreters gain a better understanding of visitors, improved communication can be achieved. Since we prefer to think

of people as an integral part of most park systems, and to consider
their behavior "natural," the bulk of the research reported here
might be considered a "natural history" of visitor groups.

This natural history approach has guided our research since
1974. We began by describing various visitor groups because so
little descriptive information was available. By documenting the
unique characteristics of a user group, we were able to recommend ways interpreters could "connect" with particular audiences.
By describing certain behavioral regularities common among groups,
we could make suggestions for improving interpretive programs
for all visitor populations. We have collected a representative
sample of such case studies, along with additional materials, so
that the reader can discover as we did how behavior patterns of a
group can become a central planning tool or focal point for a
program of interpretation.

The collective effort here represents only a modest beginning.
We have emphasized description and have been eclectic in our
selection of articles. We hope to provide interpreters with insights
into the patterned ways people behave in public recreation places,
and how those patterns can be captured within the process of
interpretation. As interpreters and social scientists together under-
take more systematic examinations of visitors, sociologists may
learn more about human behavior in parks and interpreters may
be able to see more directly the links between interpretive programs and the people they serve.

Several individuals have been especially helpful in reviewing
earlier drafts of *On Interpretation,* including William Burch, Jr.,
Sam Ham, Claire Harrison, Kenneth Harrison, Rick Schreyer, and
Ron Thoman. The Divisions of Interpretation and Visitor Services
and Science and Technology, Pacific Northwest Region of the
National Park Service, have consistently supported our research.
The many NPS employees who have attended our courses at the
Albright Training Center have, over the years, stimulated us to
learn further about people and parks. Jean Matthews initially edited each chapter with an enthusiastic yet efficient hand. Jeff Grass
of the Oregon State University Press has been a pleasure to work
with, and his editing and suggestions have greatly improved our

work. Joan Klingler has been an untiring assistant—researching obscure citations, typing, retyping, corresponding with authors— all with a cheerfulness that is much appreciated.

GARY E. MACHLIS
University of Idaho

DONALD R. FIELD
Oregon State University

CONTENTS

INTRODUCTION

At first glance, sociology and interpretation may seem strange bedfellows. Interpreters have long been intimate with the natural sciences—biology, geology, botany, ecology, and so forth. These sciences—biology and geology especially—have provided information for countless interpretive programs, from beach walks illustrating ecological principles to exhibits describing the theory of plate tectonics. Interpreters have also been intimate with the humanities—art, music, literature, philosophy, and history. Both natural science and the humanities provide the facts, and in many cases, the inspiration for interpretation.

What about the social sciences, of which sociology is only one? Social because they deal with relations between people, and science because they adhere to the scientific method, these disciplines have not often been directly applied to interpretation. Yet they offer a critical third kind of knowledge: insight into the human context of interpretive activities, facts about the interpreter and audience, and inspiration for the process of interpretation.

The Ideology of Interpretation

Interpretation is largely a service for visitors to parks, wildlife refuges, museums, zoos, aquariums and other such leisure places. Its practical objectives are straightforward—to assist the visitor, to accomplish management goals, and to promote public understanding and appreciation (Sharpe 1982). Its techniques reflect the range of communication media, from simple storytelling to complex, computerized visual displays.

Interpretation's *essence,* if we may borrow from Freeman Tilden, is much more difficult to describe. What is its role in society? What is its method—how does one *do* interpretation? What is its vocation, its central purpose? To answer these questions, we turn to Tilden as a central figure in interpretation's development.

1

Freeman Tilden was born in 1884, worked at his father's small-town newspaper, and then served as a reporter on papers in Boston, Charleston, South Carolina, and New York City. He then began a literary career, writing fiction for magazines, theater, and radio. At the age of 59 he again changed careers and began work for the National Park Service. Tilden wrote several books on interpretation, among them *The National Parks, The Fifth Essence,* and *Interpreting Our Heritage,* first published in 1957. He died in 1980. *Interpreting Our Heritage* has remained a classic work, widely acclaimed as expressing the "ideology" of interpretation.

Tilden saw interpretation as a new kind of public service, one that had "recently come into our cultural world." Sporadically practiced by great teachers, explorer-naturalists, scientists, and others, interpretation had simply been part of their role as educators. From 1915 to the 1940s, the increasing popularity of interpretive activities among park visitors and its usefulness to management agencies brought it to the foreground. Organizations from the National Park Service to local museums recognized interpretation formally and established interpretive positions, responsibilities, policies, training programs, and so forth. In sociological terms, interpretation had been institutionalized. Tilden considered this a novel development.

> We are clearly engaged in a new kind of group education based upon a systematic kind of preservation and use of national cultural resources. The scope of this activity has no counterpart in older nations or other times (1977:9).

The institutionalization of interpretation required that some agreement be reached as to its *method.* As sociologists use the term, method differs from technique; it refers to underlying principles rather than devices, skills, or practices. To Tilden, the method of interpretation was to reveal "a larger truth that lies behind any statement of fact." An interpreter could not simply recite the facts; the facts had to reveal a larger concept. Tilden elaborated in *Interpreting Our Heritage,* suggesting principles that still claim a consensus among interpreters.

If "the work of revealing" was interpretation's method, its *vocation* was revealing for a higher purpose. Tilden was neither ambiguous nor objective; there is a moral quality to his admonition that interpretation is for the enrichment of the human mind and spirit.

> The appeal for a renaissance of the appreciation of Beauty—in the abstract and in its particular aspects—must not be allowed to falter. It is vital to our moral growth. It is a program of education. Perhaps it is truer to say that it is a program of re-education, for we have always known, in our innermost recesses, our dependence upon Beauty for the courage to face the problems of life. We have let ourselves forget. *It is the duty of the interpreter to jog our memories* (emphasis added; 1977:115).

The audience is critical to interpretation, and Tilden saw that appealing to the public's interest was a necessary part of the interpreter's craft. He also knew that understanding visitors and their backgrounds was essential to the interpretive method.

> The visitor is unlikely to respond unless what you have to tell, or to show, touches his personal experience, thoughts, hopes, way of life, social position, or whatever else. If you cannot connect his ego (I use that word in an inoffensive sense) with the chain of revelation, he may not quit you physically, but you have lost his interest (1977:13).

Tilden realized that social conditions influenced interpretation's effectiveness, arguing that tourists are limited by time, "absorptive capacity," and money. Yet he shied away from any kind of analytical or systematic approach to understanding visitors. Uncharacteristically, he did not call for a foundation of empirical facts or for research on visitors.

> A roster of the reasons why people visit parks, museums, historic houses and similar preserves, though a fascinating excursion into human psychology, need not detain us here ... I go upon the assumption therefore that whatever their reasons for coming, the visitors are there (1977:11).

In part, Tilden's stance may have been due to the lack of factual information about park visitors. *Interpreting Our Heritage* was written a year before a federal commission was appointed by President Eisenhower to gather such data for the first time. Little was known about the public to be served, other than the personal experience gained by each interpreter.

Now, twenty-five years later, an immense amount of information is available to the interpreter. Studies that deal with parkgoing, environmental education, interpretation, and leisure number in the hundreds. There is on the one hand a valuable information base, and on the other an increasing "need to know." How can sociology help?

What is Sociology?

The social sciences include a range of disciplines, from anthropology to psychology. Among them, sociology focuses on the interactions among members of society. The sociologist asks: how do we behave with and toward one another? How do we organize ourselves? What meanings do we attach to the things we do?

Perhaps one of the most cogent and careful descriptions of sociology comes from the work of Max Weber (1864-1920). Weber's ideas have remained central to sociological theory and practice, and he has been called the "as yet unsurpassed master of the science of social analysis." To Weber, the fundamental value or essence of sociology is its reliance on the scientific method. The sociologist should examine how people behave in the real world and not be detoured by personal biases. Facts are to be used in testing clearly stated hypotheses. Sociology deals with what *is* rather than what *ought to be* or *might be*. Such a task demands that the sociologist distance himself or herself from the subject of interest, to be a "disenchanted observer."

Yet at the same time, studying human behavior requires the sociologist to develop special skills in analyzing what is observed. Peter Berger has written:

> While Weber was undoubtedly committed to the scientific rationality of the modern West, he had a distinctive understanding of what this meant for the study of human affairs: human phenomena don't speak for themselves; they must be *interpreted* (1981:10).

This idea, that social action must be interpreted, is at the core of a Weberian approach to sociology. Weber notes:

> The term "sociology" is open to many different interpretations. In the context used here it shall mean that science which aims at the

interpretive understanding of social behavior in order to gain an explanation of its causes, its courses and its effects (quoted in Freund 1968:93).

Hence, the sociologist is faced with not only predicting how we behave, but providing a deeper understanding as to why we behave as we do. This is partly because the importance of social behavior lies in its "meaningfulness to others." Let us take hiking for example. Two hikers may accidentally collide on a narrow trail; it is only when they ignore each other, apologize, or argue that social behavior begins. To Weber, the meaning of such social acts may vary; the crash may not be accidental, but an act of anger, or flirtation. The sociologist must go beyond simply reporting a collision and probe its meaning.

To sociologically understand our hiker's collision, we must first gather a variety of empirical facts: Who was involved? What were their backgrounds? What occurred prior to and after the incident? At the same time, the sociologist must objectively begin to probe for meanings. We might learn about other hiking encounters, looking for a pattern of behavior leading up to each collision. We might ask why the hikers did not avoid each other, or whether it is customary to collide in such situations.

By continually using empirical facts to generate understanding and then testing such understanding against more facts, the sociologist moves toward a scientific knowledge of human behavior. That is, simply, the vocation of sociology.

If the vocation of sociology is to interpret social interaction scientifically, its application has been equally broad and far-reaching. Sociologists have studied complex organizations—corporations, bureaucracies, churches, armies, factories, hospitals, and so forth. They have studied special events—pilgrimages, wars, holidays, riots—and details of everyday behavior in public parks, at school, at home, and on the job. Sociologists have examined the behavior of small groups, families, communities, nations, social classes, and civilizations. Sociology has been applied to understanding the problems of inequality, public health, racism, sexism, poverty, environmental pollution, delinquency; the list could easily go on. The intent of this book is to illustrate still another application— sociology's usefulness to interpretation.

Sociology and Interpretation

So we return to our original question concerning interpretation as it is practiced in parks, preserves, museums and similar settings: how can sociology help? Sociology can aid interpreters' understanding of their clientele. Imagine a newly developed nature center or museum located near a major metropolitan area. Who is likely to use this new facility? What occupational, educational, ethnic and religious backgrounds might the visitors have? Will they be rich or poor, young or old?

Sociological surveys, census reports, and community studies can provide this kind of information and help construct a descriptive profile of the local population. They might reveal a larger Hispanic population (should bilingual programs be considered?) or a nearby neighborhood of elderly Polish-Americans (would a special exhibit or an ethnic food festival be attractive?). Beyond this statistical profile of the entire community, the interpretive staff may need to understand the behavior of those who attend their new programs. Why are some audiences responsive and others unruly? Would evening programs be well attended? Does the seating arrangement matter? These are uniquely sociological questions, and their answers are needed to truly meet Tilden's expectation that interpreters "connect" with visitors.

Second, sociology can help us understand the process of interpretation. The interpreters at our new nature center will soon question (or have questioned for them) the meaningfulness of their work. What role does interpretation play in a citizen's visit to the site? Can interpretive programs increase visitors' knowledge, alter their behavior, or affect their attitudes and values? Or less abstractly, can the staff's interpretive programs attract an audience, increase visitor's enjoyment, and protect cherished resources? Again, these are sociological questions, and their answers are crucial to an objective appraisal of interpretation's importance.

Sociology can also help us understand interpretation as an institution and a profession by commenting on interpretation's role in wider society, describing changes in the work force, and examining interpretation's relationship to other elements of natural and cultural resource management. For our nature center's interpretive staff to understand better their organization is to be better able to work within it. Sociological studies that deal with management, training, evaluation, and supervision will prove useful to them.

Lastly, sociology can offer the interpreter an attractive "way of seeing," for the sociological perspective is compatible with the interpreter's craft. Both interpretation and sociology require curiosity about the world and society. Both are based on empirical facts, and both respect the scientific method. Both Freeman Tilden the interpreter and Max Weber the sociologist saw their professions as requiring something more—a willingness to interpret what was observable.

About This Book

The articles collected in this book reflect a narrow kind of sociological perspective. Our approach is Weberian; it is interpretive sociology as discussed above. While sociology can deal with individuals, small groups, formal organizations, and social institutions, we have focused on social groups—such as an organized tour for foreign visitors, or a family at a campfire program. Our rationale is provided in the first article, "Visitor Groups and Interpretation in Parks and Other Outdoor Leisure Settings."

In addition, almost all the articles reflect "applied" sociology—research conducted for a client and for a purpose in addition to the growth of scientific knowledge. The purpose may be to solve a management problem through interpretation, to provide interpretive planners with background information, or to help train interpreters in working with new kinds of visitors. Hence, the studies include a good deal of practical information and, in some cases, specific suggestions for improved interpretive programs.

The book is divided into three sections. Section I, "Toward Theory and Technique," introduces the interpreter to sociological concepts and methods applied to interpretation. Section II, "Case Studies" includes a set of studies conducted in the Pacific Northwest between 1974 and 1981. In addition to demonstrating empirically the diversity of park visitors, these case studies illustrate the potential contribution sociology can make to interpretation. Section III is called "Essays." The four articles deal with a range of contemporary issues important to interpretation and will, we hope, provoke the reader to apply the sociological perspective in the future.

Section I

Toward Theory and Technique

Theories have several functions in science: they explain things that are already known, predict what is unknown, and suggest lines of further inquiry. A sociological theory may attempt to explain why a certain pattern of social structure and behavior occurred or predict under which conditions similar events might take place in the future. For sociologists, theory guides their research efforts and places them within a body of previous studies. For interpreters, knowing the most useful questions to ask about their audiences may be a critical job skill. In short, theory helps organize our curiosity.

By labeling this section "*Toward* Theory and Technique," we hope to suggest that sociological research dealing with interpretation has yet to arrive at either a unified set of important questions or a wide range of understood and practiced research techniques. Clearly, interpreters can benefit from learning about people, human behavior, and the environment. The behavior of visitors at interpretive centers, for example, does not arise in isolation but is guided by the culture, community, and group of which each individual is a member. A 15-year-old male may behave differently at a local historic site depending on whether he arrives with parents, church group, street gang, or girlfriend. Theories about behavior in public places and social group processes have importance for interpretation.

The first article in this section, "Visitor Groups and Interpretation in Parks and Other Outdoor Leisure Settings," takes this perspective. Its argument is the organizing principle for this book:

9

"Effective interpretation requires a working knowledge of clientele groups." By stressing the importance of social groups, the article points the way toward applying sociological theory to interpretation. The direction, we hope, is toward a consideration of what classic sociological theory can offer. Simmel's work on small groups and Goffman's ideas about public behavior are examples.

As theory guides the questions asked, technique guides the way questions are phrased and shapes possible answers. We do not propose new strategies for interpretive research, for there are many available and underutilized research techniques. We do suggest that interpreters can benefit from a working knowledge of research methods. The interpreter so equipped can discuss with the sociologist the objectives of a research project, the kinds of data that can be generated, the reliability of the data, and the limitations inherent in any study. The interpreter can independently critique the usefulness of research reports, journal articles, and statistical summaries. And in many cases, interpreters with a basic understanding of research techniques can collect valuable sociological data themselves.

The second article, "Alternative Strategies for Studying Recreationists," provides an overview of social science techniques, from observation to surveys to experiments. As the author points out, the choice of research techniques must reflect the purposes for which the information is being collected. Interpreters who often plan, supervise, or conduct such studies should find the article a helpful guide.

Visitor Groups and Interpretation in Parks and Other Outdoor Leisure Settings

Donald R. Field
J. Alan Wagar

FROM THE VIEWPOINT of society, the objective of all resource management is to create and maintain a flow of benefits for people. Clearly, resources must be protected if they are to provide a continuing stream of benefits, but we must not lose sight of the fact that the management and stewardship of resources are for human benefit. Resource managers, however, have too seldom concerned themselves with people. Instead, they have concentrated their attention on the dynamics of the physical resources under their jurisdiction.

The limited view of resource management has worked fairly well for managers concerned primarily with material products such as wood and beef, which can be removed from their place of production and consumed elsewhere. Managers of such products seldom meet the consuming client groups. However, for parks and other recreational and esthetic resources, the final products are human experiences that are produced and enjoyed at the same location.

By adopting what we consider a mistaken view of their responsibilities, resource managers have neglected human response to resources. The physical environment is only one element affecting the quality of these experiences. Of equal and sometimes overriding importance are the visitor's values, preferences, attitudes,

Adapted with permission from "People and Interpretation," by Donald R. Field and J. Alan Wagar. *Journal of Environmental Education* 5:1 (1973): 12-17.

perceptions, and social group. These in turn depend greatly upon past associations and experiences with natural areas.

A Basis for Interpretation

An understanding of individual behavior and group influences on behavior is especially important for personnel responsible for interpretation. Interpretation includes naturalist talks, exhibits, audiovisual programs, labeled nature trails, brochures, publications, and other facilities and services which are provided to help people enjoy and understand the natural and cultural resources of the areas they visit. Effective interpretation requires a working knowledge of clientele groups for whom the messages are directed so that appropriate means can be used to arouse interest and effectively transmit information.

Interpretation can raise the quality of visitor experiences, and it is one way land management agencies can increase the flow of benefits they provide to the public. Interpretation can also increase benefits indirectly by providing an understanding of resources, perhaps leading people to support the management and more prudent use of resources.

We view interpretation primarily as the successful transmission of information to clientele groups. Facilities and methods are simply means to accomplish this end. Consequently, instead of beginning with a technique—like a visitor center, amphitheater, or other familiar interpretive format—we need first to define our objectives. Second, we must evaluate alternative procedures for reaching those objectives. Only then are we in a position to select the procedures for interpreting specific attractions or ideas for specific kinds of visitors or visitor groups. We must not simply rely on a limited set of time-honored techniques without examining their current relevance to diverse visitor publics.

Therefore, in this article we will focus on two components of interpretation: the client, and procedures for transmitting information. We will draw on current knowledge about human behavior in leisure settings to suggest alternative interpretive strategies.

Unfortunately, interpretation often falls far short of its potential for enhancing visitor experiences. Major problems diminishing its effectiveness include:

Inadequate emphasis on interpretation in resource management agencies. Do resource managers overlook the benefits of interpretation and thus allocate insufficient human and physical resources to interpretive programs? Do we recruit, train, and encourage top-flight personnel for interpretive positions?

Misallocation of effort. Do we interpret at times and places suited to our visitors? Do we present the same information repeatedly to the large percentage of repeat visitors?

Working against usual behavioral patterns. Do we utilize intragroup communication or work against it?

Inadequate attention to visitor motivation. Do we consider how interpretation will reward our visitors or only what we think should be communicated and how it should be communicated?

Mismatching of messages to visitors. Do we recognize the diverse ages, backgrounds, and interests among our visitors or do we aim at a "standardized" visitor?

Not monitoring the effectiveness of our efforts. Do we clearly state what we hope to accomplish with interpretation? If objectives are clear, what feedback mechanisms do we use to diagnose how well our interpretive efforts are accomplishing these objectives?

Although research on visitor groups and interpretation is relatively new, results already suggest alternative strategies to current management practices. It is convenient to organize the search for viable alternatives around five principles.

1. Visitors and leisure settings are diverse, and a variety of approaches will be required.
2. Visitors anticipate a relaxed and enjoyable atmosphere.
3. Interpretive information must be rewarding to visitors.
4. Interpretive information must be readily understood.
5. Feedback (i.e., communication from visitors to the interpreter) is essential.

What follows is a discussion of interpretive options. Some are new; others are being employed successfully in a variety of places. Each is related to one of these principles of interpretation.

Although it would greatly simplify interpretive planning if all information could be directed in a standardized format to the "average" visitor (a mythical character who does not exist), visitors differ widely in age, educational attainment, interests, and goals to be achieved within a natural leisure setting. Many come only to enjoy a social outing, but nearly all visitors' experiences are influenced to some degree by sociability. The goals and objectives of recreationists are partially shaped by the frequency with which they visit a recreation site. Many of those who are familiar with a specific park seek experiences that build upon knowledge from previous visits.

While outdoor recreation areas do attract new visitors each year, a majority of the visitation which occurs consists of repeat visits by groups who attend regularly (Field 1972). Therefore, a reexamination of interpretive strategies is suggested. A seasonal as well as within-season rotation schedule might provide repeat visitors an opportunity to enjoy a greater variety of interpretive experiences. One reason for the disproportionate number of newcomers found in visitor centers might be that repeat visitors have previously viewed the displays and thus spend little additional time there. Many repeat visits are by residents of the immediate vicinity. Therefore, interpreters might consider having local residents plan and maintain one exhibit which is changed periodically. A theme might be park and community history, or park-community cultural and natural events.

If exhibits and displays were self-contained and movable, they could be modified with ease. Following a modular unit idea, a visitor center could be changed periodically to update the content, adjust it for the time of year, or provide variety for repeat visitors. Modular units would likewise offer staff members an opportunity to test, evaluate, and modify a proposed design prior to embracing it as a permanent part of their interpretation. In addition, modular units could be rearranged to accommodate different traffic flow patterns as visitor numbers change during different parts of the season. Exhibits might also be made modular in a slightly different sense. Equipment for presenting slides synchronized with sound is now available in a variety of forms. This allows quick substitution of one program for another, permitting presentations to be tailored to the needs of the moment. An interpretive staff could use flexibility of exhibit content, design, and spatial arrangement as additional means for enhancing message reception.

Too often we find interpreters assigned to visitor contact areas where only a small proportion of the total visitors can be found. Rotating staff assignments to areas of visitor concentration might be required. An examination of interpretive emphasis (where and to whom and at what time) is needed. One might develop a balance sheet to assess where the visitors are and where interpreters are assigned. Sightseeing by vehicle, for example, is one of the most popular activities in parks. Interpreters who are available along major road systems have a greater contact opportunity. Interpreters on public conveyances such as buses likewise contact more visitors. Camping is a popular activity, and campgrounds are a traditional interpretive site. Yet very seldom do we find interpreters in campgrounds in the morning, midday, or afternoon. Because picnicking is the third most popular activity in parks, picnicking areas could be used much more widely for interpreting natural and cultural features.

People usually visit recreational areas as members of social groups. Patterns include family groups, friendship groups of the same age, and groups of different ages. Although most resource managers recognize that people come to parks with others, such managers often do not understand the social group's influence on the perceptions, attitudes, and behavior of individual members (Field 1971). Because so many of the visitors reached by interpretive programs arrive in social groups rather than as individuals, the social group is an important vehicle for the transmission of interpretive messages. One important aspect of group behavior is its role in shaping information for children of different ages. At the same time, group members who assume leadership roles as teachers or interpreters, rather than passive listeners, tend to gain improved understanding of the information they present.

We must also provide opportunities for the group to gather together to share information being received. For example, relief models that show the topography of an area are among the most popular exhibits in visitor centers (Washburne 1971). One reason for this popularity is that they readily accommodate groups. When gathered at a relief model, members of a family or other group can discuss information of interest among themselves and can set their own pace.

Visitors consider parks and other outdoor leisure settings to be places where informality prevails and group members are free to interact. Unfortunately, a great number of interpretive facilities are now designed to deal impersonally with individuals as individuals, without allowing any opportunity for group interaction. Thus, in the press of serving increasing numbers of people, informal campfire programs have become formal lectures to large audiences seated in neat rows. Instead of a real live naturalist, many visitors meet only audiovisual programs and message repeaters.

We recognize that budgets for interpretation severely constrain the amount of face-to-face interpretation that can be offered. However, informal contacts with interpreters are in many cases the most rewarding for the visitor and should be encouraged to the greatest extent possible. In amphitheaters, for example, fixed benches might be replaced with less formal seating patterns, and the interpreter might move among the visitors while presenting his topic. By avoiding a stage as much as possible and allowing for periodic interruption and questions from visitors, he might create an atmosphere which encourages informality and participation.

As part of their informality, parks and other outdoor leisure settings are places where it is considered appropriate behavior for strangers to interact. This may be unique to leisure settings and should be encouraged (Cheek 1971a, 1972). Interpretive planners might capitalize on both this informality and the diversity among visitors by hiring interpreters of various age groups who could initiate informal interpretive happenings. For example, in the Southwest where many retirees visit parks, a few should be hired to specialize in informal interpretive contacts with others of the same age. Their discussions of opportunities for retired visitors could focus not only on park attractions but on the recreational and social opportunities available for older citizens in nearby communities. In other settings where teenagers are predominant visitors, selected teenagers might be employed to present interpretive information to their own age group. The familiarity of retired and teenage interpreters with the life style of their peers might make them especially effective at involving segments of our society often neglected in specialized presentations. In both cases, qualified people might well be available on a volunteer basis.

People tend to persist in doing the things they find enjoyable and rewarding. Yet this has often been overlooked in interpretation, especially among interpreters who have strong preconceptions about what people ought to know or ought to find enjoyable. For example, Graves (1972) protested the use of tape players, movies, and exhibit systems designed for participation. If, however, we want to enhance the quality of people's experiences and want to help them understand the attractions they visit, we had better reject notions that the only worthwhile visitors are those whose values duplicate those of the professional resource manager.

Our research has demonstrated a number of factors that contribute to visitor interest in interpretation. One of the most important is to provide for visitor participation and involvement. For example, at the Ohanepecosh Visitor Center in Mt. Rainier National Park, we installed a recording quizboard that simply presented four written multiple-choice questions and permitted each to be answered by pushing electric buttons opposite the answers selected (Wagar 1972b). When a correct answer button was pushed, a green panel reading "right answer" lighted up, the question panel just answered darkened, and another question panel lighted up. In addition, the quizboard made a rather satisfying clicking sound as relays snapped and as hidden counters registered people's answers. Although the other exhibits in the visitor center were extemely well done, the quizboard was the only exhibit that permitted participation and manipulation. Within seconds after it was installed, it became, for children, the most popular exhibit in the center.

We might further harness the "kid power" of participation which also increases the retention of information received. Ecological float trips, for example, have been initiated at Yosemite National Park. Other possibilities might include organized bike trips to interpret a particular topic. An organized game of litter removal can be more than a cheap way to clean up areas; it can be an interpretive device to instill a philosophy for "keeping America clean" (Clark *et al.* 1972). Interpretive programs for children only, combined with an activity like roasting marshmallows (again employed at Yosemite National Park) and puppet shows or reading of stories based on ecological principles, are other examples.

To capitalize on the principle of visitor participation, living demonstrations should be encouraged like those which show eighteenth century life patterns at Colonial Williamsburg. In addition, opportunities for visitor groups to engage in an activity like painting, shooting a musket, or "throwing" a pot might be developed where appropriate to the social, cultural, and natural history of an area. Nothing is more convincing to the novice regarding the skill required to create some object or the significance of a period in history than watching his family or friends recreate the object or event.

A study of exhibits at five different visitor centers showed additional factors that were rewarding to visitors (Washburne 1971). Holistic presentations that included cause-and-effect relationships were found to be more interesting to people than isolated facts. As for subject matter, violence and violent events were of greater interest than all others (which seems to have been well known by writers and entertainers for thousands of years). Fortunately, leisure settings abound in examples of violence that can be interpreted in good taste. For example, life in the ocean is so hazardous that, for most organisms, millions of young must be hatched to insure that a few will survive to maturity.

Interest was far above average for exhibits with such dramatic or animated presentations as movies, changed lighting (to direct the visitor's attention from place to place), and recorded sound. By contrast, interest was below average for such inert presentations as texts and mounted photos. Viewed another way, visitors find the media normally used for entertainment more rewarding than the less dynamic media traditionally used for education (Travers 1967). As media commonly associated with entertainment, television, tape recorders, and radio have all been employed one place or another with varying degrees of success. However, their full potential has not been exploited.

Closed-circuit television offers enormous possibilities, especially now that relatively inexpensive videotape systems are available. For example, one interpreter at a central control unit might interact with visitors at a number of monitors. By talking to visitors at any monitor, he could determine their interests and levels of knowledge, answer their questions, and then show them a videotape while interacting with other visitors on other monitors. Where the construction of a theater in a visitor center would be questionable, television might offer a less costly alternative.

Portable cassette tape players also offer great flexibility. During a recent study visitors were able to choose tapes of different lengths for a nature trail (Wagar 1972a). The choice could have been extended to tapes with different emphases, different levels of difficulty, or even different languages.

Short-range radio transmitters are now being used in parking lots at a number of places to contact visitors through their own car radios. Use of transmitters at intervals along a road has also been considered as a means of presenting a sequence of information to visitors as they drive along. Costs per visitor contact appear to be quite reasonable. At the moment, however, it is not certain that available equipment will provide adequate range from a simple antenna without exceeding the power output permitted for unlicensed transmitters. New limits for power output currently seem to be under consideration by the Federal Communications Commission. At a substantially higher cost, cables can be laid under the roadway to control the transmission zone.

In addition to making interpretation rewarding, interpreters must use language readily understood by the visitor. For ready understanding, the terminology, examples, and analogies used for interpretation must be within the vocabulary and experience of the visitor. Ideally, examples should draw upon situations and experiences well known to the visitor. For example, it would be foolish to compare a smell to the aroma of new-mown hay for visitors whose olfactory environment has included mainly factory smoke.

In addition to easily grasped language and examples, understanding depends on prior knowledge. To understand how DDT can threaten brown pelicans with extinction, one must understand food chains and the mechanisms by which DDT is passed along from species to species in increasing concentrations. To understand a geyser, a person must recognize that the boiling point of water increases with pressure.

Where pamphlets or brochures are needed, as at park entrances or nature trails, they might well be written in several versions. A variety of styles could be employed, oriented to different visitor publics. Different versions or sections might assume different levels of prior knowledge or might be aimed at different age or interest groups. The National Park Service already has some materials for children, describing natural or cultural features in story form and including pictures which can be colored. This provides an excellent way to orient children to natural resources. A question-answer series that encourages parents and children to interact while discussing a park or recreational feature would also reinforce the natural parent-child relationship in family units. If planned to accommodate diverse groups of visitors, pamphlets or other material would better serve new visitors, repeat visitors, youth, retired visitors, or even visitors who do not speak English.

Perhaps no general concept or principle is more important for interpretation than feedback. In general terms, feedback is simply a set of signals indicating the extent to which an operation is going as planned and showing what corrective action would be useful. For interpretation, feedback is a flow of information from the visitors that lets the interpreter know how well he is achieving both his objectives and those of the visitors. Because different visitors will have different objectives, feedback is essential for tailoring presentations to a variety of people.

When an interpreter meets face-to-face with small visitor groups, feedback is readily available. Unless he is totally insensitive, the interpreter can tell from people's expressions, questions, and other behavior if they are interested or disinterested and if they understand his words and examples. Using this continuous flow of feedback, he can continually correct his presentation to increase its effectiveness.

Once the easy and informal exchange of face-to-face interpretation is lost, obtaining feedback becomes more difficult. Instead of direct interaction with a good cross-section of visitors, the interpreter is increasingly exposed to fellow interpreters, to visitors who are especially receptive to interpretive presentations, or to visitors who are too polite to criticize shortcomings. More than one interpreter has had his bad habits perpetuated by insincere compliments.

The use of feedback to evaluate effectiveness must be based on clearly stated objectives. Surprisingly, many interpreters and interpretive planners cannot specify exactly what it is they are trying to do. To be useful, objectives must be taken beyond vague generalities and stated in terms of behaviors the visitor could express as a result of interpretation (Mager 1962). An objective that lends itself to evaluation would be to enable the visitor to describe food chains in general and the particular food chain which permits solar energy to be utilized by the cave cricket.

Once clear objectives are defined, feedback procedures can be devised to monitor the effectiveness with which objectives are being accomplished. These procedures can range from the interpreter's informal collection of impressions during face-to-face contact, to suggestion boxes, to formal studies in which visitors are asked to indicate how enjoyable they found interpretation and are then tested on their understanding of the information presented. Such a test would pass or flunk the interpreter, not the visitor.

To avoid the many problems of attitude measurement, evaluation should be concentrated on objective information (Hendee 1972b). Not only are attitude changes difficult to measure, but attitudes are unlikely to change much due to the short exposure provided by most interpretation. It is far better to measure effectiveness in transmitting basic concepts. If people understand these, their attitudes and behavior are quite likely to shift in appropriate directions.

Ideally, feedback mechanisms should be designed directly into interpretive programming. The recording quizboard mentioned earlier is simply a device to determine how well visitors understand ideas presented to them. It lends itself especially well to determining whether a change in interpretation is increasing or decreasing comprehension by visitors. Currently, there are audio-visual exhibits that intermittently present the visitor with questions and record his answers. This equipment not only shows how well different kinds of visitors are understanding a presentation, it also permits interpretive presentations to be tested in a mock-up stage without great cost. Such testing is a valuable indicator of success or failure. If the interpretation is not understood, the fault usually is with the presentation, not the visitor. An added feature of experimental audio-visual equipment is the fact that it can be programmed so the visitor's responses determine the level at which additional information will be presented, permitting a wide range of visitors to be served by a single system. When integrated into interpretive progamming, feedback procedures can permit the diagnosis of effectiveness and can indicate opportunities for improvement.

A central premise of this article is that the objective of all resource management is to create and maintain a flow of benefits for people. Resource managers, however, have often emphasized resource protection or manipulation, without clear recognition that such efforts are a means to an end for parks and similar resource areas where human experiences are emphasized. This view is not only inappropriate but can lead to a misconception of visitor objectives and a narrow view of what is considered appropriate human behavior in leisure settings.

Resource managers responsible for interpretation must understand both human behavior and resources sufficiently to inform and enhance experiences for various visitor publics. Five principles of effective interpretation have been suggested: 1) visitors are diverse, 2) visitors anticipate a relaxed and enjoyable atmosphere, 3) interpretive information must be rewarding to the visitor as well as to park management, 4) interpretive information must be understood, and 5) the effectiveness of interpretation must continually be evaluated. Furthermore, the objectives of interpretation need clear definition prior to the selection of an interpretive method or format.

Alternative Strategies for Studying Recreationists

Roger N. Clark

UNDERSTANDING RECREATIONAL problems and the motives, preferences, values, and behavior patterns of recreationists is an important concern for recreation managers and researchers. Such understanding is essential for identifying the consequences of alternative recreation management strategies.

Because recreation researchers have a variety of social research tools available, care must be taken to ensure that the chosen study procedures are consistent with the subject matter to be studied. Accurate, unbiased information is essential for the development of effective recreation policies and management schemes, and it is the urgent business of recreation planners, managers, and policy makers to be just as concerned as are investigators that the research programs used are appropriate to the study and rigorously applied.

This article describes alternatives to the traditional cross-sectional survey and presents a framework for selecting when a specific data collection strategy may be appropriate or inappropriate. The framework allows the researcher to examine the alternatives in terms of the information they can and cannot provide. Such a framework should also prove useful to planners, managers, interpreters, and policymakers, because it gives a basis for evaluating whether the data developed in a study answer specific questions about recreational phenomena. The aim is to provide a general overview of when and why each approach may be best.

Adapted with permission from *River Recreation Proceedings,* U.S. Forest Service General Technical Report NC-28. St. Paul: North Central Forest Experiment Station, 1977. The advice of Dr. Thomas Heberlein, University of Wisconsin, during the preparation of an earlier draft of this article is gratefully acknowledged.

Basic Research Questions About Recreational Behavior

Two fundamental types of questions that researchers and policymakers might ask about recreation behavior are 1) questions requiring description and 2) questions requiring explanation.

Description

Good description is the key to understanding and is often neglected in social science research. Three basic descriptive questions for which researchers or policymakers might seek information are:

What is happening, when, where, and how much? Answering this question involves a basic description of the event being studied. For example, the researcher may want to know how extensive visitor use is and how it varies from location to location or by time or season.

Who is involved? Describing the social, physical, and psychological characteristics of the persons involved in the event under investigation will answer this question. For example, who visits an interpretive center? The young? The old? The highly educated? Groups or individuals?

What do people prefer? Most people make a variety of choices daily in keeping with their personal values and goals. Describing the various preferences for types of recreation—for example, what visitors consider desirable developments or acceptable management procedures—is central to both understanding and providing for recreation opportunities.

Explanation

After a phenomenon has been adequately described, the next step is to explain why it occurs. Two general questions relating to the explanation of a phenomenon are:

Why is it happening? This involves an explanation of the phenomenon in terms of either participant motivation or various components of the environment. For example, can visits to a specific park be explained by the user's desire to be there, or by the fact that few alternatives exist for that kind of experience?

Why do people choose one area over another? Why do they violate well-posted rules?

How can behaviors be modified or changed? Answers to this question are often necessary for producing desirable results in recreation areas as well as other places. Changing (or maintaining) a certain behavior is often the desire of the resource manager who may be faced with problems of overuse, litter, vandalism, sanitation, conflicting uses, or intolerable resource damage. Information provided in answer to the earlier questions is often essential in preparing a study to answer this final question. Examples include: How can litter or vandalism be prevented, and what procedures will effectively disperse visitors along popular interpretive trails?

Research Designs
And Data Collection Strategies

In preparing a study to answer one or more of the above questions, the researcher must choose from a variety of research designs and measurement strategies. A research design is the basic framework within which data are collected. The researcher must decide whether data about the same population will be collected only once (cross-sectional design) or more than once (longitudinal design). Or does the investigator hope to determine cause-and-effect relationships through some control procedure (experimental design)?

Measurement strategies are the various procedures by which data are collected. Does the researcher look for himself (observation) or are subjects asked to speak for themselves (self reports)? Any study is a combination of a research design and measurement strategy (e.g.) a cross-sectional survey or a longitudinal observation study) or an experimental design using direct observation as a measurement strategy.

Research Designs

Cross-sectional. This design is characterized by one measurement of the phenomenon in question across a segment of the target population. It allows for intersubject comparisons of the characteristics or behaviors measured.

Longitudinal. This design (also known as panel or time-series studies) allows for measurement of attributes or behaviors within a target population two or more times. It allows for intrasubject as well as intersubject comparisons over time.

Experimental. This design is characterized by some sort of manipulation or control procedure by the investigator and an evaluation of its effect on the phenomenon in question. Did the manipulation result in any change in attitudes or behavior?

Measurement Strategies

Observation. Observation refers to systematic techniques for observing, recording, and evaluating behavior. Such observation follows specific procedures and is much more exhaustive and objective than casual observation done in the course of normal events by both managers and participants. There are three methods for observation: direct observation of events as they occur, observation of traces of behavior, and participant observation.

Self reports from subjects. The subjects under study can be asked to report the desired information to the investigator. Essentially, this requires the subjects to "observe" their own characteristics, behavior, or feelings about what they do or events that go on about them. The tools used in this approach are surveys (interviews or questionnaires) and diaries.

Advantages and Disadvantages
of Alternative Research Designs
And Measurement Strategies

From the researcher's perspective, answers to all five basic research questions are important for an understanding of a particular recreation phenomenon. Practically, however, some questions may be more important than others. Managers, for example, often are concerned with maintaining or modifying certain behaviors. Unfortunately, no single combination of a research design and measurement strategy will provide data to answer these questions. The method of study must be selected with two criteria in mind: Will it provide reliable and valid information to answer the questions directly? Will it provide the information efficiently?

Table 1 summarizes the relationships between the basic questions and alternative research designs and measurement strategies. The basic assumption is that the design and measurement strategy is acceptable *only* if it can provide valid and reliable data to answer the question directly. Therefore, conjecture and inferences based on data collected to answer other questions may not be appropriate for judging the utility of the method under consideration, particularly if there is a better alternative. Readers should refer to Table 1 during the following discussion about the advantages and disadvantages of alternative research approaches.

Research Approaches for Questions of Description

The Cross-Sectional Survey

The cross-sectional survey is the standard social science tool used in most recreation research. Indeed, it is the most common method used in all social science research. The pros and cons of using this method are presented first to serve as a baseline for comparing the other methods.

Three kinds of information are typically sought in a survey: 1) Respondents are asked to recall their past behavior or to predict future behavior (e.g., how many trips they've taken to a certain historic site). 2) Respondents are asked to report descriptive characteristics such as income, education, age, sex, place of residence, and similar items. 3) Respondents are asked to report individual psychological states, attitudes, preferences, and beliefs about such things as wilderness, rivers, recreation, and society. Examples would be survey items like "I believe there is a crowding problem at this park," or "I prefer solitude at my campsite," or "I think people should pick up the litter of a friend." Each of these types of information is examined below.

Behavior recall. Behavior recall is often used in surveys to answer the questions, "What is happening?" and "What is preferred?" Because of the serious shortcoming of this approach, behavior recall is a poor substitute for other methods. Behaviors recalled on a questionnaire or interview are likely to be an inaccurate measure of actual behavior. In studies of littering, for example,

Table 1. Relationship of research designs and measurement strategies to basic questions about recreational behavior

| | Basic questions about recreational behavior | | | | |
| | Description | | | Explanation | |
	What is happening—when, where, how much?	Who is involved?	What is preferred?	Why is it happening?	How can it be maintained or modified?
Research designs					
Cross-sectional	X	X	X	(X)	
Longitudinal	X	X	X	(X)	
Experimental			X	X	X
Measurement (data collection) strategies					
Observation:					
Direct observation	X	X	(X)	X¹	X¹
Trace observation	X	(X)	(X)	X¹	X¹
Participant observation	X	X	X	X	X¹
Self Reports:					
Behavior recall surveys	(X)		(X)		(X)¹
Surveys of reported characteristics		X			
Surveys of reported attitudes, beliefs			X	X	
Diary (log)	X	X	(X)	X	(X)¹

¹ Appropriate within an experimental design
X = Acceptable alternative—provides data to directly answer the question
(X) = Acceptable under limited conditions

more than 50 percent of people observed littering said they had not (Heberlein 1971).

Several factors probably account for the discrepancies observed. A common human frailty is our inability to objectively record our own behavior, even under the best conditions (Mead 1964), and particularly the motivations behind our behavior. People may simply not know or may forget what they did or when they did it. They may think events happened more recently than they actually did. Definitional problems also may operate; when asked how many times one has visited rivers in wilderness areas, a person may count trips to areas which really aren't wilderness. And, as in the case of not reporting littering behavior, people are reluctant to admit illegal or inappropriate behavior and therefore may deliberately mislead the investigator.

Reported characteristics. Asking subjects to report various personal or group characteristics is straightforward and is usually a part of most surveys. Requesting this information is usually secondary to asking about their behavior or attitudes. Many personal characteristics, although not reported without error, are sufficiently accurate for most purposes, especially when the high cost of determining such information by other means is considered.

Reported characteristics gathered through a questionnaire or interview describe many unobservable as well as observable variables related to individuals and groups ("Who is involved?"). Whether or not this measure of "who" is appropriate depends on how involvement in the event under study was determined. If involvement is based on self-reported behavior recall data, then relations between "who" and "what" may be questionable. If, however, the investigator has some prior knowledge about actual involvement in an activity (direct observation, use registers, licenses, etc.), the sample can be restricted to those known to be involved in the event of interest. Such a description of "who is involved" is more likely to be accurate than one based purely on self-reported recall data. Generally, the results of broad surveys directed at an unidentified population must be viewed with caution.

Reported attitudes, preferences, and beliefs. Most surveys focus on respondents' attitudes, preferences, and beliefs. This approach is not without serious problems, as has been well documented in the social science literature (Heberlein 1973). Attitudes are conceptually complex and difficult to measure. An attitude survey often appears easy to carry out but in fact requires a great deal of skill in conceptualization, measurement, and analysis (Potter *et al.* 1972).

Further, it sometimes appears that attitude studies are done when people are really interested in behavior, and the implicit assumption has been made that attitudes closely approximate real behavior. But, there is little evidence of a direct effect of attitudes on behavior (Deutscher 1966; Hancock 1973; Heberlein 1973; Wicker 1969). Wicker's study showed that attitudes predicted real behavior only 10 percent of the time .

A basic question for which attitude studies are appropriate is, "What do people say they prefer?" From a carefully conducted attitude survey of the appropriate population, a manager may accurately assess what people say they prefer. Stankey (1973) showed how wilderness purists prefer different wilderness management policies than nonpurists do. He argued that such preferences should be taken into account in wilderness management.

Attitude studies allow people to assess and consider hypothetical alternatives which do not exist. However, this hypothetical nature of the alternatives presents its own difficulties. We may be developing and managing recreation areas on the basis of hypothetical answers to attitude questions not representative of the real world.

Alternative measurement strategies

Self reports—diaries. This self-report procedure requires that participants record their own behavior, feelings, etc., as close to the time they occur as possible. As the name implies, diaries are kept over an extended time period, such as a float trip down a river. Respondents may be asked to record their motives for doing things as well as what they did. Diaries are particularly useful for gathering information about people while they are traveling to remote locations such as along rivers or when their travel prevents easy observation. The reduced time lag, compared with that of surveys, compensates to some extent for the inaccuracy of behavior recall described earlier.

The diary approach has many of the faults of other self-reporting procedures. For example, only normative behavior is likely to be recorded completely and accurately. Inconvenience also may prompt incomplete entries. Even with its faults, the diary is a procedure that must be considered when information over a period of time is wanted. With proper instructions to the respondent, many of its shortcomings can be reduced.

Diaries can be useful for determining "what is happening." Diaries have been successfully used by state fish and game departments to study fishing and hunting activities and by researchers to study wilderness travel (Lime and Lorence 1974). Diaries should include appropriate instructions on what to record, how to enter information, and when to log the entries. Diaries are best used when the investigator can specify things he wants documented, for example: "When and where did you camp?" "Who were you with?" "What did you do in the evening?" "How many other parties did you encounter?" Requesting that "everything you do" be recorded, over even a short period of time, is usually unworkable and puts an unnecessary burden on the respondent.

Diaries can yield accurate information about "who is involved" in an event. This information about "who" is similar to that provided on questionnaires and interviews, except that the information is presumably recorded as the events occur rather than recalled later.

Systematic observation of events as they occur. For this form of observation, the specific events or objects under study must be well defined and directly observable. This technique can be used by an observer who tallies specific events or notes certain objects by some prearranged coding schedule. Or it can be done by artificial surveillance such as remote cameras and other automatic recording devices. This approach can be used to study the amount and type of use an interpretive facility, area, or trail receives.

Systematic observation of actual behavior in recreational settings has several problems. First, the measure may be reactive; that is, the presence of an observer may affect the behavior under study. For example, measuring littering behavior by placing observers along a trail is likely to reduce incidence of the behavior, because people tend to litter more when they are alone (Heberlein 1971). Therefore, even if observations of behavior are reliable, they may be invalid because of the reactive distortion caused by the measurement process itself. A second and more serious problem for the outdoor recreation researcher is that systematic observation of actual behavior may be inefficient and expensive, because some behavior is difficult to observe or seldom occurs. In remote settings it may take many hours to record a few observations because of infrequent and scattered use. A third concern regarding systematic observation is observer reliability (Burch 1974). Without specific training for the observer, pretested recording schedules and instructions, and continual reliability checks, a serious distortion of actual events can result. Indeed, the observer is both the strength and the weakness of this approach (Kerlinger 1973).

When events are well defined and directly observable, systematic observation will produce reliable, valid, and accurate results about "what is happening"—if the problem of reactivity can be overcome. A definite advantage of this procedure is that with proper sampling, generalizations can be made about specific individual and collective behaviors.

Systematic observation of events can also describe "who was involved." Variables such as the subject's sex, race, age, etc., can easily be recorded at the time the event is observed. The only criterion is that "who" be clearly identifiable.

Systematic observations of events as they occur can sometimes provide data to answer the question, "what do people prefer?" For example, observation focusing on where people choose to camp along a certain river may reveal a preference for locations far from other sites. However, the correlation between the presence of other sites and actual preference may be spurious. Perhaps the locations were selected because of some other quality, such as availability of sunlight or nearness to a good landing. Some other procedure (such as a survey or diary) will be necessary to clearly establish the reason for the choice.

Systematic observation of behavioral traces. Observing the effects of previous behavior may be appropriate in some cases. Observation of traces is one way to reduce costs of direct observation and to obtain nonreactive measures, because the subjects under study need not be present when data are collected. Webb *et al.* (1966) described a wide array of such unobtrusive measures.

Accretion or buildup of environmental factors caused by human behavior are a good measure of such behavior. For example, how much litter accumulates at historic sites? Although these measures may be unreliable because of weather factors, they are generally useful and relatively inexpensive. Measures of the degradation or erosion of the environment also are useful. The rates at which trails are wearing down or firewood and foliage are disappearing are measures of the amount of use an area receives. A wide array of such traces may be regularly recorded in and around a recreation area by the creative investigator.

An important difference between traces and other measures of behavior is that traces usually indicate aggregate behavior rather than individual behavior. This limits the generalizations that may be made from the resulting data. When individual events need not be or cannot be observed directly to determine "what is happening," measuring their traces may be useful. By systematically observing the accretion or degradation of a variety of factors that occur as a result of recreational behavior, a measure of its impact can be determined. Such aggregate data may be sufficient for planning and policy purposes.

Trace observation can yield information about "who was involved," although validity and reliability must be seriously questioned. The presence of discarded fish bait containers and fishing gear wrappers suggests that fishermen were in the area; the presence of horse droppings or feed hay at campsites suggests that horse users were there. The precision with which such data can be measured, however, may limit its usefulness. And, because traces are a measure of aggregate rather than individual behavior, the investigator cannot determine from the above example if fishermen or horse users were the only people in the area, or if the fishermen came on horseback. Interpreting and generalizing such data are difficult, but for some purposes, the knowledge that fishermen or horses were in the area may be enough.

Use of traces to determine "what is preferred" suffers from all the shortcomings of direct observation, plus those inherent in measurements of accretion and degradation as reflectors of previous events. This method should be used only when alternatives have been ruled out.

Participant observation. As Campbell (1970) points out, participant observation is more than a single method of data collection and may include a variety of techniques for gathering quantitative and qualitative data. This method is unobtrusive and relatively inexpensive. Some writers include systematic observation as a participant observer's role (Campbell 1970; Gold 1958). Discussion of this procedure is limited here to roles involving interaction with participants. That is the essence of participant observation, and the thing that distinguishes it from the other forms of observation.

The method is difficult to define simply, but it generally involves the investigator directly taking part in the activity he wishes to study. The observer is able to observe his own reactions to events taking place as well as reactions of others. Through this interaction with participants and continual data processing and evaluation, the investigator can reformulate the problems as the study proceeds and look for new information (Dean *et al.* 1969).

Major disadvantages of participant observation include the possible lack of objectivity and reliability of the observer, the possibility of becoming overwhelmed with large amounts of information, reactivity if the identity of the observer is known or suspected, and information that may be subjective and incomplete. Systematic theory testing requires more rigid procedures.

Participant observation is often useful as a prelude to surveys or more systematic counting of objects, specific events, or behavioral traces. Operating as both observer and participant, the investigator can gain insights that otherwise might not be apparent. Participant observation is an excellent and efficient tool for defining the dimensions of a program, because it can quickly generate a great deal of diverse information.

In the early stages of a study, participant observation is useful for determining "what is happening" at a broad level—the range of events, types of participants, activities, problems, etc. A major advantage of this method is that the observer is often able to gain access to events because he is involved in them and does not pose a threat to people being observed.

Participant observation gives a clear picture of "who is involved" in events that the observer sees. Finding out who was engaged in events not observed is also possible by talking with others. The participant observer often has access to information about "who is involved," because he is more readily accepted as a member of the group than a formal observer or authority. Thus, data on "who" result from what is seen and what is learned from others.

Participant observation should also be considered an important alternative in the study of "what is preferred," particularly in the early stages of an investigation. The observer learns about preferences by several methods—his own and other people's choices (for example, where to camp within a park) and informal talks with them to determine what they prefer. Initially, participant observation may help determine the range of preferences, but a more systematic process would best detemine their relative importance.

Alternative research designs

Longitudinal design. In addition to the problems with the survey measurement strategy, the cross-sectional design of many studies limits the generalizations that can be made from the data. With events measured only once, intersubject comparisons can be made across the population at that time only. With a longitudinal design (measurements of the same population two or more times), both intersubject and intrasubject comparisons are possible over time, and descriptive questions can be more readily answered. As an alternative to the cross-sectional design, longitudinal design of studies can clearly identify trends over time, if disadvantages of the measurement procedure are considered. Longitudinal designs, however, impose greater burdens on both researcher and subject because data are collected more than once (Crider *et al.* 1973).

Experimental design. In essence, an experimental analysis is a longitudinal design with some manipulation occurring between measurements. Data are collected by observation or a self-reporting procedure. The element of manipulation and before and after measurements make this process unique. Although few experiments are reported in the literature on recreational behavior, many experiments are actually done but without sufficient documentation to determine effectiveness. In day-to-day decisions, managers and policymakers initiate changes in recreational environments that may have some effect on people. For example, they may provide trash cans along a river, build a new road for boat launching, develop more campsites, add convenience facilities, or restrict access.

The manipulation or change is essentially the guts of an experiment. The impact of the change needs to be evaluated so that the desired results will be attained. More attention should be paid to documenting the cause-effect relationships implicit in most management actions to ensure that undesirable consequences do not occur. For example, as Clark *et al.* (1971) illustrate, the process of "creeping campground development" in response to increasing use may have serious effects on the types of users attracted to certain areas.

An experimental design may be useful for providing data on "what is preferred." Direct observation, and to some extent self-reports (even if done within a longitudinal design), will provide partial answers on how people behave or their stated preferences. However, these approaches may have serious flaws. To determine exactly which factors influence choice implies some sort of experimental design. By systematically controlling or manipulating characteristics of campsites, for example, and measuring the effect, researchers and managers could identify important factors related to site preference and use.

Research Approaches for Questions of Explanation

The Cross-Sectional Survey

The cross-sectional survey may be suited to answer the question of "why things are happening," particularly when the answer may require a social-psychological explanation. A carefully conducted survey of attitudes can explain why the phenomenon occurred in terms of the social psychology of the action and the mediating decision process. To do a study of attitudes presumes that one knows a great deal about the process itself, but many attitude studies seeking to learn why something is occurring don't seem to have this understanding. Such studies are marked by a wide variety of unrelated questions, the lack of clear research hypotheses prior to data collection, and the general sterility of results. Further, when trying to explain why a behavior is occurring or how to control it, an attitude study may be inappropriate; situational or environmental factors may be largely responsible, and these are generally ignored in most surveys.

The cross-sectional survey is inappropriate for determining "how a behavior can be modified or maintained." Research on litter control by Keep America Beautiful, Inc. (1968) presents a good example. Respondents to a survey identified two classes of reasons for littering. The first class included individual attributes—laziness, indifference, carelessness, etc. But this description doesn't really tell us why littering occurs, because these data say nothing about the process linking such attitudes to littering behavior. The second class of reasons relates to situational factors—trash facilities, litterbags, etc. The problem here is that littering itself was not under study. Respondents were asked to give reasons why they think littering occurs or how it can be controlled. Whether or not facilities, laws, litterbags, and education had anything to do with the respondents' past, present, or future littering behavior cannot be ascertained from this type of study. Indeed, other research (Clark *et al.* 1972a; Heberlein 1971) suggests that laws, educational campaigns, and trash facilities have little impact on littering. And all these studies focused directly on the problem—littering and litter.

Alternative measurement strategies

Self report—diaries. Diary studies can provide information on "why a behavior is occurring" if respondents describe why they did what they did. For example, when boaters choose among streams in an area and locate their movement on a map, the investigator may want to know why they made their decisions. Reasons may include "this way was shorter," "too many people the other way," etc. This approach, however, has all the weaknesses described for the use of diaries to answer descriptive questions.

Participant observation. Participant observation can answer the question of "why a behavior occurs"—both from the point of view of the observer, who may engage in the event and record his own reactions to it, and from the perspective of those he observes. The observer interacts with other participants and is often able to learn "why" through conversation. Measurement of "why" with participant observation procedures is most useful in the early stages of a study; it can help the researcher ask the right questions later on. Participant observation is often necessary for a good attitude survey. It should be noted, however, that although participant observation may be necessary for an attitude study, it is not a sufficient replacement for such a study. Participant observation provides hypotheses, but only the carefully conducted attitude study, with its systematic sample and rigorous measurement, provides strong support for hypotheses dealing with social-psychological explanations of "why."

Alternative research designs

Longitudinal design. When the investigator wishes to determine if the reasons "why an event is happening" change over time, then a longitudinal design may be appropriate. This is a particularly useful approach when combined with a survey aimed at determining social-psychological reasons.

Experimental design. If the factors controlling a behavior are situational, experimental analysis can yield data about "why it is happening." For example, use of a visitor center may be related to access, visibility, proximity to other sites, etc. Experiments can isolate the relative impacts of the various factors.

Experimental analysis is the only method that allows the researcher to determine directly "how a behavior can be modified or maintained." Although a simple observation of behavior and cognitive explanations of why it occurs may provide insight into possible control procedures, any testing of the effectiveness of controls implies an experiment. Research on litter control in recreation is an example of how experimental analysis can be used to determine effective control procedures (Clark 1976; Clark *et al.* 1972a; Heberlein 1971). A carefully conducted experiment is the key to determining the effectiveness of management actions, because the relative impacts of each approach can be clearly substantiated.

Related Issues

A variety of research designs and measurement strategies have been presented here within a simple framework for determining which may be appropriate for providing information about several questions concerning recreational behavior. The decisions that must be made about appropriate strategies are more complex than the framework implies. Several important related issues that the investigator should consider in designing a study will now be discussed.

Variety of Procedures

When used alone, none of the strategies described can produce data to answer directly the five basic questions about recreational behavior. Consequently, researchers interested in all of the questions must be able to use a variety of research designs and data collection strategies. Rarely will one of the five questions be studied alone; usually, a study will combine several. This makes it particularly important for the researcher to understand the limitations of the alternative procedures and to select the combination that best satisfies the study objectives.

Appropriate Research Strategy

The appropriate research strategy may depend on what is known about the events of interest to the researcher or manager. Studying a phenomenon about which little is known may require a different approach than if specific variables have been identified. Participant observation is particularly useful in early stages of an investigation and can be used to focus data on four of the five basic questions. More information is required to use the other strategies; systematic observation requires identification and definition of important variables; self reports require the right questions for pertinent responses; and experimental analysis requires identification of target behaviors and possible controls.

An effective overall approach is to focus initial data collection efforts on participant observation to identify variables that can be more accurately measured by systematic procedures. By considering what is known and which of the five basic questions should be studied, the researcher can determine the most appropriate research strategy.

Practical vs. Scientific Importance

An important concern, particularly to data users, is whether the information to be collected will have any practical importance. Consequently, both the researcher and practitioner must understand the implications that the data collection strategy has for potential application. Does the researcher want to study questions of most importance to the manager? If so, the choice of strategies is limited to those best suited to producing valid and reliable data that will directly answer questions of interest.

Conclusion

Attitude studies (primarily cross-sectional surveys), if done carefully, can play an important role in answering major questions about recreation and recreationists. They are particularly useful in explaining why certain events occur. They also give the most systematic information about what people say they prefer (although experiments may give a wider range of choice and tell more about what people actually prefer in certain settings). Attitude studies, however, seem to be done to the exclusion of both observational studies and experiments. Such a strong reliance on this technique limits the ability to increase our knowledge about a variety of recreational phenomena.

There are several possible explanations for the strong reliance on cross-sectional surveys. First, many investigators incorrectly feel that they have a good idea about what is actually happening when beginning a study. Hence, there is a tendency to neglect the basic descriptive questions and move directly to research that will explain the phenomena. Or investigators may think, inappropriately, that behavior-recall data from surveys will describe adequately what is happening and who is involved.

Another reason many investigators focus on attitude surveys is that they believe attitude studies really tell how behavior can be changed. There are strong reasons for disagreement with this point of view. It is experimental analysis focusing directly on behavior (or attitudes, if that is what one wants to change) that can do this. This problem, coupled with the poor relationship between attitudes and specific behavior, indicates that more time should be spent in direct observation or experimentation with the behaviors in question.

Finally, most social scientists conducting research on recreation are trained in survey methodology and often are not familiar with other alternatives. Consequently, this strategy is often used when other procedures would be more appropriate. All recreation researchers, regardless of academic background, need a thorough understanding of the alternative procedures available to them.

Regardless of the reasons, it seems clear that social science efforts in studying recreation, regardless of the setting, need to be refocused. The consequences of not doing so are great, particularly when the data have policy implications. Determining the best strategy for collecting data depends on a variety of factors discussed in this paper. Individual researchers need a basic understanding of *all* the strengths and weaknesses of each strategy.

Section II

Case Studies

The case study has long been a traditional technique of sociology. By focusing attention on a particular person, group, or institution, the case study allows the subject to be examined in some depth and with the kind of special insight not available with other methods, such as the sample survey. Hobbs and Blank write:

> One case study by itself cannot prove much of anything. But if there are many case studies that tend to agree and that tend to provide insights to more general conditions, then sociologists are on the road to a generalization that could prove significant (1982:18).

Hence, case studies usually have broken new ground, exploring for the first time a variety of "cultural scenes." Classic sociological case studies include vagabonds (Anderson's *The Hobo*), pool hustlers (Polsky's *Hustlers, Beats and Others*), working-class men (Whyte's *Street Corner Society*), ethnic groups (Leibow's *Tally's Corner*), and communities (Warner's *Yankee City*).

The case studies in this section share several things. First, each deals with a specific clientele group found in parks and other interpretive settings. Individual chapters deal with children, families, senior citizens, foreign tourists, and cruise ship travelers. These chapters are modest efforts to show examples of research on social groups of interest to the interpreter.

Second, the predominant research technique used in most of these case studies was participant observation—the researcher observing behavior in the field. Bultena *et al.* observed senior citizens at over one hundred interpretive programs, and the study of family camping involved two and one-half months' field work.

Exceptions are the chapters on children and foreign tourists, which are descriptive accounts based on data collected for other purposes. Each of the case studies attempts to link description with practical suggestions for improved interpretation.

A third similarity is that these case studies were conducted in the Pacific Northwest. Locations included Mt. Rainier, Olympic, Crater Lake, and North Cascades National Parks, as well as the waterways of Southeast Alaska. The Northwest is a unique region; it has relatively few ethnics, few blacks and Hispanics. Its cultures are young, and its land is largely under federal ownership (67 percent of Idaho is federally owned). Except for the Seattle area, its economy is predominantly based on primary production— timber, fish, agriculture, mining—and tourism.

Many of the basic visitor behaviors and organizational forms described in these studies (as in the discussion of four family types) are undoubtedly found in other parts of North America. The general social processes described by Koth *et al.* as occurring on board Alaskan cruise ships are very likely repeated on board cruise ships sailing the Caribbean from ports on the industrialized East Coast. Yet the reader is well advised to pay attention to what is similar, what is different, and what is impossible to generalize from these case studies to other settings and regions.

Finally, all of the case studies offer evidence for the diversity of visitor groups suggested in earlier chapters. Machlis found, for example, that treating families as a unique visitor public was an oversimplification. He describes the behavioral differences among family types as significant in their impact on the use of interpretive services. Whether it be children at different stages of development, Japanese visitors on a package tour, or retirees traveling the "snowbird circuit," these case studies illuminate the rich variety of social groups that form the interpreter's audience.

Getting Connected: An Approach To Children's Interpretation

Gary E. Machlis
Donald R. Field

> ". . . to find the human key to the inhuman world about us; to connect the individual with the community, the known with the unknown; to relate the past to the present and both to the future."
> P. L. Travers, *Only Connect*

WHILE THERE ARE various definitions of interpretation, most agree that either the transmission of information to visitor publics or the stimulation of a desire to acquire information is a key aspect. Simple as it may sound, matching an interpretive approach and material with the appropriate audience is perhaps the most difficult challenge facing those responsible for the array of public contact programs.

All too often the audience has been taken for granted, misread, or incorrectly identified. Elsewhere several writers have indicated that the manager's conception of the visitor, who he is, and what he seeks in recreational places *differs* from what the visitor assumes about himself and from what the visitor actually seeks in leisure places (Clark *et al.* 1971). This finding is perpetuated by the mass-oriented interpretive programs prevalent in many recreational places, which assume that all visitors are alike. But all visitors are *not* alike. Instead a *diversity* of visitor groups can be found in recreational places like national parks. The interpretive programs offered also must vary in intent, content, and approach (Field and Wagar 1973).

Adapted with permission from "Getting Connected: An Approach to Children's Interpretation," by Gary E. Machlis and Donald R. Field. *Trends* 7(1974):19-25.

The bases for assessing differences are numerous. Visitor publics vary in terms of the frequency with which they come to parks and in their previous experience with outdoor leisure places. Perhaps the most obvious difference among visitors is their age. Yet an assessment of programs offered reveals a low number of interpretive options specifically designed for either the young or the old.

This article is directed toward one segment of the visitor public—children. Its purpose is to aid in "connecting" interpretive programs with them. Getting connected requires:

1. An understanding of the developmental phases of childhood growth and how they offer opportunities and limitations for children of various social and chronological ages.

2. Consideration of the importance that group life has on children and how social groups can affect interpretation.

3. An understanding of three basic interpretive approaches that should be central to any program dealing with children.

Any fruitful approach to children's interpretation must have a conceptual framework soundly based on the way children behave. Interpreters may ask, "Under what conditions will a particular program be exciting and effective for children?", or "How can we design an interpretive program for schoolage youngsters?" The answers lie in understanding human behavior.

When examining children's interpretation, it is useful to think in terms of communications flow. To be connected with children, the message must pass through the interpreter, the medium of communication being used, and the social situation in which it is being delivered—all before it reaches the child. Each of these factors can potentially encourage effective interpretation or discourage such efforts. If the message is incomplete, the interpreter inarticulate, the equipment jammed, the screen torn, or the room lighting too bright, immediately there are barriers to communication. If the social environmnent is inappropriate, the message may not be received. If the child is not developmentally mature enough to participate at the level of an interpretive program, getting connected is extremely difficult. Hence, understanding the behavior of youngsters in each developmental phase will help in providing interpretation that truly connects with the young visitor.

How Developmental Phases Affect Interpretation

This same sort of negative/positive potential can be of value in looking at the phases of childhood development. In each phase, certain characteristics can act as limitations on getting connected, while others can act as motivators. *Children's interpretive programs need to exploit those characteristics that act as motivators.*

> Example: If five-year-olds learn primarily through the sense of touch, then interpretive exhibits that allow tactile responses will motivate these children. Exhibits labeled "don't touch" will limit their own effectiveness.

In discussing developmental phases of childhood, many cautions must be observed. These phases are purely conceptual, and no child goes to sleep one night in the latency period to awake as a preadolescent. Rather, there is a continuum of development wherein physical, emotional, and cognitive changes gradually occur. These changes happen at different chronological ages from child to child and vary from generation to generation. To further complicate matters, children may be in transition from one phase to the next, or may just be developing at a slower chronological rate.

For the preschooler, who is cognitively just beginning to make associations of cause-and-effect, interpretation of simple natural relationships can be exciting. Preschoolers have abundant energy and large active movements. Their interest span is short, so interpretive programs should be constructed in small sequential units. They are primarily self-centered and work better individually. The preschooler is concerned with scales: "big and small" are important concepts.

> Example: An interpretive program that involves the children physically in a "miniature ecosystem" running and climbing up small valleys and along creeks and streams. There are natural places to hide, logs to cross, and all at a scale appropriate to the children.

At about five years of age, the child enters what can be called the schoolage phase. Cognitively, comparison becomes a prime mode of analyzing information. Interpreters have assumed that schoolage children are interested in factual data concerning natural history: "The tree is 110 feet tall." However, the interest may be not with the data as such, but in how this particular tree measures up to the tallest tree in the area. Comparisons can make data come alive for the schoolage child. The schoolage child is only tentatively beginning to form relationships with adults outside the family, briefly leaving the protection of the caring person, usually the mother. Physical growth becomes more gradual.

Physical growth continues into the preadolescent phase, which begins around the age of nine. There is wide variation in development from child to child, with interests and curiosities varying even more. The preadolescent is beginning to enjoy group life and is finding parent substitutes in teachers and group leaders. The credibility of the interpreter in the eyes of the child becomes extremely critical. There is a striving to attain skills and a concern with things rather than ideas.

> Example: A "living history" program where groups of children could learn about frontier baking by grinding flour, stoking the oven, and eating the final product.

This concern for things rather than ideas changes as the adolescent phase begins, at about twelve to thirteen years of age. At this stage, a desire arises for intellectual freedom and for authentic information with which to make independent decisions. The adolescent is struggling for independence, yet critically needs peer group approval. An interpretive program that allows for teenage leadership and self-discovery is apt to be more effective than one based on adult supervision and fixed rules.

> Example: A program of volunteer environmental cleanup projects, bringing trash back from high mountain country; or teenagers leading younger children on interpretive walks.

The first goal in getting connected is to use the motivators inherent in each developmental phase to best advantage.

Children and Social Groups

More than any other segment of our society, children participate in interpretive experiences while in a group. A family may
visit an interpretive center, a school class may take a trip to an
historical site, or a group of campers may go for a nature walk
around camp. Central to understanding child behavior is the social
context in which interpretation takes place. One cannot effectively develop interpretive programs for children without understanding the dynamics of children's groups. Like the concept of
developmental phase, social context can act as a limitation or a
motivation in connecting the message. What are some of the
variables affecting the social context of the children's interpretive
programs?

The purpose of the group

Before other questions are addressed, it is useful to consider
the basic purpose of any children's group. The purpose may be
education, recreation, entertainment, or simply delivery of an
agency message. The group may be used to offer new experiences
to the young or to supervise and control behavior.

Also, it is important to ask who defines the purpose of such a
children's group. Little league baseball is an example of a children's
group whose purpose is largely defined by adults. Children quickly
learn the real purpose for their group's existence and often act
accordingly.

> Example: Is the campfire's purpose to present an agency message and
> supervise children, or to teach environmental concepts and give kids
> a chance to relax and enjoy themselves?

Group size

Group size is an important factor. Active outdoor games may
be motivators for large groups of early schoolage children and
indoor activity may be severely limiting.

> Example: It is unreasonable to plan a structured, passive program for
> large groups of eight-year-olds. They have incredible amounts of
> energy, are intensely physical, and desire attention from adults. Non-
> constructive chaos is almost inevitable.

Group composition

The composition of the children's group also defines social context. Since the interpreter often has little control over group composition, interpretive programs must be flexible to adapt to changes in group composition. We need to ask if the children in a particular group are currently in different phases. Or, as is more likely, are some in a specific phase and others in transition? Will these differences affect the group and its purpose?

Other variables need to be examined also. What is the social and educational background of the children? The proportion of males to females becomes crucial in the preadolescent phase and continues to influence behavior into adulthood. Partly because of urbanization and the decline of open space in urban areas, interpreters must be aware of the environmental experience of the children. How many different environs has the group been exposed to, and in which settings are they motivated or limited? Children of the city cannot be expected to spontaneously relax and enjoy wilderness environments without previous successful experiences. Fritz Redl speaks of urban children's summer camp experiences:

> City children have heard and read about storms, animals, and nature and have used these images as props in their nightmares and daydreams. What isolated contacts they have made with nature usually were in broad daylight or in the protective custody of father or mother on that car trip. Suddenly all nature is let loose on the child from town; the result is that many children are frightened at camp much of the time (1966:441).

The effective interpreter will consider these variables in planning and conducting interpretive programs.

> Example: A group of young scouts is preparing for its first campout. It is obvious to the adult leader that while most of the group enjoys group life, several "loners" are involved. The leader offers responsibility for keeping a journal of their trip to several of the loners, giving them the very needed chance each day to relax from the requirements of group life inherent in scout trips.

The second goal of getting connected is to use the social context of the group as a motivator.

Interpretive Approaches

The next step in getting connected is to examine various interpretive approaches. An interpretive approach should not be confused with a medium such as films or the written word, or with schedules of interpretive activity. Such an approach is a way of programming built upon three basic modes of human expression: action, fantasy, and instruction.

Action

Children learn by doing. They learn physical skills such as skipping and throwing by imitation and repetition. They want to be able to do things and are not truly content with being told how or shown. An impatient "Let me do it!" is a signal to the interpreter that his interpretive approach is ignoring this important mode.

Action is valuable in the development of other kinds of skills. Participation in an activity offers children practice in interacting with others, and helps them to empathize with other's emotions—an important part of what adults consider maturity. Indeed, sometimes the only way for a child to understand how another feels may be to act out the role.

> Example: An interpreter is explaining to a group of schoolage children that for the pioneers coming west on the Oregon Trail, winter was a hard time. The children do not react. The interpreter asks them to act out winter on the Trail, without fresh food, warm clothes, or adequate shelter. The play acting goes on for about five minutes. The interpreter then continues his story, carrying along with him the children's interest and understanding.

Fantasy

Perhaps the most powerful and far-reaching mode of interpretation is fantasy. Fantasy is an intimate, personal, and imaginative thing. To the child there is a potential for fantasy within every experience. Indeed, when modern children are confronted with a basket woven by Native Americans hundreds of years ago, we are inviting them to fantasize about a life and culture far different from their own. Interpretive displays that encourage fantasy can spark interest and involvement, even though the display itself may be quite static. Yet while the children are so involved in fantasy, it is seldom openly used by interpretation planners and programmers. And why not? C. S. Lewis notes:

> He (the child) does not despise real woods because he has read of enchanted woods: the reading makes all woods a little enchanted (1969:215).

Instruction

Instruction is by far the most accepted and expected mode of interpretation. It is the main way we teach children in our schools, and whether by slide show, campfire talk, or museum exhibit, one-way communication of information is the most prevalent method of interpretation.

For youngsters the importance of information is directly related to its usefulness.

> Example: To know how to identify Oregon Grape may be mildly interesting, but the information comes alive when it is made known that the berries can be used to stain decorations onto cloth.

To be valuable, instruction should concentrate on providing information that can be directly incorporated into the lives of children.

For children, these modes of expression are closely related, with each offering strong motivations. The effective interpreter weaves them all together, moving from one mode to the other as the individuals and group require.

> Example: A group of seven-year-olds are learning about salmon. The interpreter begins by showing the children pictures of the large fish, and asks if they have ever seen one. The children are told that salmon can often weigh nearly one-half of what they (the children) weigh. Can they imagine being such a large fish in a shallow stream? Could they show what it would be like to be a salmon swimming upstream? "What happens if there is a dam?" asks the interpreter. The children act out climbing a fish ladder, if possible on a small ladder built for such activity. The playacting goes on for several minutes. The interpreter tells the children the rest of the story about the salmon's life cycle. It is mentioned that no one understands why the salmon can return to the same stream where they began life as eggs. The children are asked: "Can you think of a reason?"

Obviously, using these conceptual tools requires a great deal of prior planning on the part of the interpreter. Given the complexity of the groups, he or she cannot be expected to utilize every possible motivator in each interpretive encounter. What is needed is a systematic planning process for children's interpretive programs.

Summary

"Getting connected" seemed appropriate for the title of this article, because many of the ideas germinated while reading P. L. Travers' article on children's literature, "Only Connect." Some important things to consider here are: the developmental phases of growth, the social context of the children's group, and modes of interpretation—action, fantasy and instruction. Books, papers, and articles that discuss these concepts can aid in getting connected. But alone, this understanding and discussion *cannot* create enjoyable children's programs. Getting connected ultimately requires creativity, love of children, curiosity, and an ability to look on the role of adult with bemused suspicion.

The Social Organization of Family Camping: Implications for Interpretation

Gary E. Machlis

Introduction

O N A SUMMER weekend almost anywhere in our country, the campgrounds are full to overflowing; trailers and tents of every description fill the many campsites. Many of these weekend shelters are inhabited by families; as family members, they build fires, make friends, and go to evening programs. This paper is concerned with family groups and how they organize themselves while camping. Using the techniques of participant observation, four kinds of families were examined—the *nuclear, multiple, extended,* and *partial* family. The objective was to discover patterns of social organization associated with the activity of camping as they might be manifested in each family type.

A family camping trip is an important event and requires social and economic resources heretofore sparsely treated in the literature of family life. To those families for whom camping is a primary group activity, participation may be critical to maintaining family ties—invaluable in a society that in many ways serves to separate family members from one another.

It is also important that family camping be understood by those responsible for the management of our country's parks, recreation areas, and campgrounds. Families comprise one of the largest categories of park visitors, and their impact on the physical and social environments of these areas may be significant. As

Adapted from "Families in the Parks: An Analysis of Family Organization in a Leisure Setting," by Gary E. Machlis. (unpub. Master's thesis, University of Washington, 1975).

families are active participants at interpretive events, describing family behavior at campgrounds may be useful to interpreters.

Methods

The study was undertaken at Mt. Rainier, Olympic, and Crater Lake National Parks during the summer season of 1974. Participant observation was used to gather data on families camping overnight in developed campgrounds within the parks. More than 74 hours were spent purely as an observer; a similar amount of time was spent participating in camping activities with family groups.

While observations were taken of both individuals and groups, the unit of analysis was the social group. Observations were stratified by family type to compensate for a preponderance of nuclear families in the campgrounds. Four family types were examined: *nuclear* (parents and their children), *multiple* (several nuclear families permanently or temporarily combined), *extended* (encompassing the kin network), and *partial* (single-parent families).

In addition to observation periods, interviews were conducted with family groups. These interviews were in-depth and informal, and questions were open-ended. Families were encouraged to speak freely and discuss their camping experiences and organization. The nonrandom sample was again stratified, so as to provide adequate data on single-parent and extended families. Photography was used to record special behaviors or events and to analyze spatial organization of campsites and camp activities.

Background

What are the key elements that make up family life in a camping setting? By describing those relevant to the *concept* of family, we can look at specific kinds of family groups through a common eye. If there are key elements that make up family life, we can try to describe how these elements operate within families in the parks. To understand family camping, we must first understand the family as a social group.

Several sociologists have attempted to lay out framework for investigating family life (Parsons and Bales 1955; Burgess *et al.* 1971). Social work researchers, concerned with the practical problems of troubled families, also have made this attempt (Geismar 1964). Burch (1964) touched upon family organization in his analysis of sex-typing in camping settings. This study of families in the parks embraced three key variables of family life: *family maintenance, family interaction,* and *family activities.*

When families go camping in outdoor recreation areas, the demands of *family maintenance* continue to shape much of family behavior. One of the primary maintenance functions is that of shelter. How is the maintenance of family shelter organized? Is the responsibility of shelter building sex-typed? How are camping shelters spatially located? Another primary aspect of family maintenance is food preparation and meals. Mealtimes require obvious organization and division of labor and therefore provide an excellent event for analysis. A third important function is protection—usually by parents and of children. This activity is highly visible in parks, especially at interest points and campgrounds that include natural hazards. How the protective function is carried out is an important element of each family's camping pattern.

Understanding *family interaction* is also critical to understanding families in parks. Meeting maintenance requirements often initiated a division of labor within the family group. Members were assigned (overtly or by norms) certain roles and behaviors. For example, fathers were often in charge of shelter building and campfires; mothers were in charge of cooking and child supervision. This division of labor formed the primary relationships and interactions within the family group. Parsons and Bales (1955) argued that there is a universal tendency toward "instrumental" roles for men and "affective" roles for women. An expanded view of role differentiation is presented by Blood and Wolfe (1971) in their work on family task performance. Blood and Wolfe argue that who does what is determined by both norms and by availability. If the normal performer is not available, then roles become more and more diffuse as tasks switch from member to member. Thus, an important aspect of family organization is how roles are assigned to family members. Do traditional sex-typed roles become more diffuse in the outdoor recreation setting? How do these roles interrelate?

Another major theme of family interaction explored in this study of families in parks is the fundamental question of group cohesion—the extent to which an individual's roles include interaction with other members of the group. Hess and Handel (1974) point out that two conditions characterize the family group; the members are intimately connected to one another, yet they are also separate. Each member must establish his or her own personality and identity and, at the same time, integrate personal behavior into that of the group. Each family must develop its own balance of connectedness and separateness.

The outdoor recreation setting is ideal for examining family cohesion, for the disruptive influences of employment often are left behind. Burch writes:

> Camping differs from other play in that the campers, though isolated from the commitments of everyday life, pursue many of the routines of everyday life. The family unit for the duration of its engagement is a relatively self-sufficient unit containing the resources of existence without immediate, direct dependency on others (1965:605).

The third major element of family life in outdoor recreation settings is *family activities,* those units of group behavior that involve all family members to one degree or another. Families' activities may be agency initiated—developed by park management for visitors—such as interpretive centers, organized interpretive trails, and evening campfire programs. They may also be park-inherent—available due to the natural features of the area—such as mountain climbing, playing in streams, and fishing. Finally, activities may be family initiated—developed by families independent of park resources—such as reading, badminton, listening to music, and so forth. Do different types of family groups gravitate toward different kinds of recreational activity? Are these activities organized in discernible patterns?

Another important aspect of family activities is their potential for ritualistic content. Bassard and Boll (1950) describe family rituals as beginning with "recurrent family behavior." As an activity is staged over and over again, definite forms of interaction and a specific cultural content are built up. The family ritual is a social process, one with the possibility of strong emotional overtones. Its importance to family cohesion is easily apparent.

Yet rituals serve other functions besides binding the family together. For young children, the material context of the ritual—the specific patterns of behavior—become pathways to social participation in the family group. The rituals become tools for the transmission of family culture. We know from previous research (Burch and Wenger 1967, among others), that childhood outdoor recreational experiences affect leisure choices in adulthood. Yet at a more psycho-social level, we are relatively ignorant of how this takes place. One possibility is that the rituals act as "culture carriers," and are reenacted (in different forms, perhaps) in adulthood. Because knowledge in this area is incomplete, an analysis of family ritual in camping settings was undertaken.

Results

The Nuclear Family

The fundamental unit of American family life is the nuclear family (Reiss 1972). Past studies of recreational use (Field 1972) have chosen not to differentiate between family types, making conjecture on the proportion of nuclear families difficult. However, it was very clear that nuclear family groups were the most common social group in each of the campgrounds studied.

The nuclear families observed in this study occupied primarily single-unit shelters—a tent, camper or trailer that housed the entire family. Occasionally, nuclear families were found using two shelters, with parents sleeping inside a trailer or camper and the children in a small tent nearby. Rather than a requirement for family maintenance, these extra units often seemed to be "adventure places" for the young.

For nuclear families, shelter building was primarily a responsibility of the father. Several fathers observed in field situations continued shelter building long after the demands of maintenance and convenience were satisfied. The tent was readjusted or the campsite reorganized. Burch (1965, 1971) describes this behavior as "symbolic labor"; such efforts also serve as creative outlets for the men who engage in them.

In the nuclear family, the protection function took two basic forms—preventive and active. Much of the protection that parents provided for young children was preventive. Campsites were chosen for their relative safety. Active protection also was plainly visible within nuclear family groups. Two important factors were evident: active protection was sex-typed as a female activity, and such protection often helped produce tension within the family.

> Father with movie camera takes pictures of daughter feeding the squirrels. Parents encourage her to feed them, while the father shoots several feet of movie film. Mother calls her back repeatedly from the lake rim. Father tells her to stay put so he can film.

> Father switches to Polaroid camera and tells her not to be afraid. The mother calls her back angrily, and finally both daughter and father come back over the rim wall (observation notes, August 24).

"Trophy-taking" (Burch 1965; Hendee *et al.* 1971) in the national parks, such as this father's attempt at filming his daughter, often involved some sort of real or imagined risk. To the extent that the urge for trophies conflicted with protection, tension was created. While trophy-taking was sex-typed as a male activity, active protection was definitely a female responsibility; hence much of the tension created was between mother and father. Another source of conflict was the close confinement between nuclear family members in their shelters.

These tensions, no doubt, appear regularly in the home. Yet part of the reason such conflicts occur in the campground is that for the nuclear family, the balance of connectedness and separateness leaned heavily toward connectedness, whole group interaction, cooperation, and family cohesion. The nuclear family when camping is concerned with togetherness, combined with sometimes opposing roles; conflict and tension are bound to occur. This orientation toward togetherness was not the case for all kinds of family groups.

Observations suggest that nuclear families are involved in all manner of activities in outdoor recreation settings. Familiarity with the park and its recreational opportunities helped determine the most frequent kinds of activities. Families that had low familiarity with a park tended to involve themselves in agency-initiated programs such as campfires, nature walks, and visitor centers; families with high familiarity (often locals) tended toward park-inherent or family-initiated behaviors. This phenomenon was repeated in several areas consistently. Family activities seemed to change as familiarity with a recreation setting increased. As newcomers gained experience, knowledge, and equipment, dependence on agency-initiated activity seemed to decline.

Multiple Families

Multiple family groups—two or more unrelated nuclear families camping conjointly—represented a discrete kind of family group observed in the study areas. Some were families who have communal living patterns at home and bring those patterns with them when they visit a park. Others were traditional nuclear families who joined together specifically for outdoor recreation. Maintaining a multiple family group may entail more adults caring for a larger number of children, and many multiple families were able to develop ways to deal with these larger numbers of individuals. Kitchen areas were larger than for nuclear families, and meals often were all-group activities.

Shelter tended to be in separate nuclear units, partly due to a desire for adult privacy and the fact that recreational shelters designed for multiple families are not readily available. The shelters usually were arranged on campsites in patterns similar to those exhibited by nuclear families, but again this may be due to a lack of alternatives. Almost always, a single campfire circle served the entire group.

The key element in the cohesion of multiple family groups was the sharing of the protective function by all adult members of the group. It was "watching out for Ed's kids" and "taking care of the Wilson boys" that enabled multiple family groups to function in the parks. Protection of children was often sex-typed as in the nuclear family. Strong discipline was left to a child's parents; shared protection did not imply complete interchangeability of roles.

Multiple families had a wide range of family activities, similar to nuclear groups. The multiple family often involved itself in park-inherent activities that lent themselves to large group participation (beach hikes, organized games). Most of these activities reinforced the cohesion of the group. Teams were never chosen along nuclear family lines; children were told to "listen to Mrs. Charles" and "do what she says."

Parent and child roles were diffused considerably in the multiple family, similar to the process as it operates in communes or other group homes. The ability to engage in adult activities and momentarily share the caring and protective function with others enabled adult relationships other than mother-father dyads to develop.

It has been suggested that the nuclear family is heavily oriented toward connectedness while camping in parks. There is also togetherness in the multiple family; togetherness is what makes communal life. Yet because of the diffusion of norms involved in such conjoint endeavors, the enforcement of a single norm for group cohesion may be somewhat less severe.

The Extended Family

Nuclear families do not exist in a social vacuum, isolated from other kin. Researchers such as Litwak (1961) and Parsons and Bales (1955), while in disagreement as to the extent of kin relations, agree that the "modified extended family" is functioning in modern America. The modified extended family is a kin network of individuals and nuclear family groups banded together by affectional ties and choice (Sussman and Burchinal 1962; Litwak 1960). Sussman and Burchinal found that the major activities linking family networks are mutual aid—both financial and emotional—and social activities. This suggests that leisure may be a major factor in extended family relationships. In fact, Dotson (1951) found that extended family get-togethers and joint recreational activities dominate urban working class leisure pursuits. Hence it was reasonable to expect extended families in the parks.

Shelter was a combination of nuclear family units and adventure places. Because of park regulations and site design, extended family shelters were spread over several numbered campsites. However, it was imperative to most extended groups to be situated as close to one another as possible. Camping "close" often meant parking recreational vehicles off designated areas; soil compaction and vegetation trampling also were prevalent.

When a large extended family took its position in a developed campground, a central campsite often became the extended family "commons." Nightly campfires, family conversations, and large group meals were often held at this site. The extended family commons became the center for family maintenance and activity and usually was accompanied by overuse of the immediate area. Sites peripheral to the commons were used to varying degrees. Most meals were taken in nuclear subgroups.

Within the extended family, protection was handled in ways similar to that suggested for multiple family groups. Protection was shared, with each adult member having a measure of parental responsibility and authority over the kins' children. Unlike the multiple family group, more parental transfer of discipline was evidenced. Older family members often "looked after" children, freeing young parents for other activities.

Many of the extended families observed were engaged in more than recreational camping. They were staging an intricate and important ritual—a family reunion. It is hard to overemphasize the importance of this change in motivation. An extended family that stages a family reunion in a park likely has developed emotional ties to the recreational area that the park, the campground, even the campsite represent. These recreational places become traditional family settings; these camping activities become family rituals. Many of the extended family reunions examined had been held repeatedly in the same place, often at the same campsite. Many return each year at a specific date. They have developed attachments to areas administered by recreational agencies that transcend the meanings that managers and casual visitors use to order behavior in the park.

Family activities for the extended kin network tended to be family initiated, and there was little participation in agency-initiated programs. Team games were popular and often carried much ritualistic content. For extended families celebrating reunions in outdoor settings, much of family activity carried with it the social weight of tradition.

As could be expected, the extended family involves a complex network of social relationships. For extended family groups that included several generations, interaction revolved around the patriarch and/or the matriarch of the clan. Relationships tended to be directed upward, with identity and status gained by generation and age. Marriage-related members (a brother-in-law or sister-in-law) had equal standing; in the families observed they were always full participants.

Competition between generations was encouraged, and most large extended families had contests of one kind or another. However, competition between members of the same generation was treated differently. Often, each member developed a special role that gave unique status. One young adult male might be "the top clammer of us all' and another "the frisbee champion." In this way, every member gained attention and status without undue family competition.

It must be remembered that while the extended family is camping in parks, the kin network is not the only social structure that affects camping behavior. Each nuclear subgroup spent considerable time with its own members, and their behavior was similar to that already discussed. The tension-producing conflict of trophy-taking versus protection was not as evident in the extended family subgroups, but this may be due more to familiarity with the park than to a unique social structure. For a family group returning to the same area many times, both the anxiety of protection and the desire for trophies may be significantly reduced.

The Partial Family

Just as membership in the family can be expanded from the nuclear group to the kin network, death, disruption, and divorce can reduce the family to partial status. Single-parent families were observed in the study areas; in-depth interviews were conducted with several such groups.

Maintaining a partial family in a national park campground requires the same basic maintenance roles as the nuclear counterpart requires. Most of the observed partial families camped in single-unit shelters. There were fewer "adventure places" for youngsters; the partial family was sheltered together. Unlike nuclear families, shelter building was decidedly not a sex-typed activity, primarily because a single parent was the family head. Blood and Wolfe's (1971) theory of availability was clearly demonstrated as the female family leader took charge of setting up shelter, and children of both sexes pitched in to help.

This diffusion of work roles was evident in other forms of family maintenance. Food preparation became a family activity, and the entire group participated. The pressures and responsibilities of protection were especially evident in our observations of partial families and interviews with single-parent families. Without another parent (and often without another adult) to help, a single parent was left to assume the entire protective function alone. The difference from the organized protection of the multiple family was striking.

Partial families were largely dependent on agency-initiated programs for family activities. Many partial families stayed close to their campsites, talking, playing cards, stoking the fire. These times were not necessarily temporal bridges between other events: sometimes the activity continued for several hours. Partial families often had low familiarity with park areas, and their dependence on agency-initiated programs limited the range of activities in which they participated. Social relationships also were somewhat limited. Without a spouse to share in the protection, socialization, and emotional support of the children, the single parent often had little chance for social contact outside of parent-child relationships.

To the partial family, the question of connectedness and separateness is fairly moot. Separateness is a fact of partial family life outside the park. Hence, inside the outdoor recreational area, partial families tended to concentrate heavily on the connectedness of family life. Unlike the nuclear family, such a concentration did not run the risk of alienating individual family members. On the contrary, partial families welcomed the chance to use camping as a means for unifying and solidifying the family group.

Implications for Interpretation

From the research just described, several general conclusions about family camping are possible. First, families can be classified into four types—nuclear, multiple, extended, and partial. Each has a distinct membership. Information that allows for the classification of a family unit is relatively easy to obtain. The typology is not restricted to recreational research but can accommodate family groups in most settings. Second, this framework is especially useful in examining family camping. Each family type has developed distinct adaptive strategies for dealing with the maintenance, interaction and activities involved in outdoor recreation, and specifically family camping.

Third, knowing into which type a family falls may help identify the social organization and behavior of that family. Knowing that a large, multigenerational extended family is about to enter a campground, we can predict the kinds of activities they may likely pursue and how the group might be organized internally. Such sociological knowledge can be useful in dealing with a range of interpretive situations. An example is the issue of protection. In protecting their young, families often had little familiarity with a park and its accompanying hazards. This left protection in the hands of park management. New ways to reinforce safety messages through interpretation that involves parents might be effective in reducing accidents within the parks.

Interpretive efforts that cater to the family group are especially appreciated by park-visiting families. For example, an interpretive program that generates dialogue between parent and child is especially appropriate for partial families; programs that provide parents with interpretive information can utilize the teacher-learner roles of parents and children. In such cases, the interpreter allows the family to interpret and acts as a catalyst for such encounters. It might even prove successful to have extended family groups and reunions present programs, encouraging visitor participation and dialogue between families within the park.

The data suggest that families having little familiarity with a recreational area are largely dependent upon the park agency to provide things to do. This needs further investigation; if it is true, there are important implications for interpreters. Some activities and written materials might be geared toward first-time visitors with the purpose of increasing familiarity; programs in areas with high numbers of repeat visitors might be altered or even discontinued.

Finally, this study suggests an intriguing path of discovery. It is concerned with how outdoor recreation fits into the general scheme of all-around family life. Are the behaviors and patterns of organization observed in campgrounds different from what goes on at home, school, or on the job? Are there behavioral differences between families that go camping and those that do not? Research that seeks to synthesize our knowledge of family camping and general family life can offer answers to these questions, and such answers may be useful to interpreters.

Interpretation for the Elderly

Gordon Bultena
Donald R. Field
Renee Renninger

THE FACT THAT the national forests and parks today are serving a diverse clientele is important to an objective appraisal of the interpretive interests and needs of visitors. It has been found, for example, that national parkgoers are drawn from all age and social-class levels, from several racial and ethnic groups, and from rural and metropolitan areas; they display widely varying levels of education, unique cultural and experiential backgrounds, and diverse motives for visiting parks (Cheek & Field 1971; Outdoor Recreation Surveys, 1968). Despite this diversity, there has been a tendency for public agencies to plan programs for the mythical "average visitor," and thus to lose sight of, and perhaps give inadequate attention to, the unique interpretive needs and interests of visitor subgroups (Field & Wagar 1973).

This paper reports findings from a study of the interpretive interests and involvement of one segment of the parkgoing public—retirees. Although older persons have been found to be less dedicated parkgoers on the whole than middle-aged or young persons, retirees who visit national parks often do so with considerable frequency and make relatively long stays. It can be anticipated that older persons will become an increasingly important audience for park interpretive efforts given their growing numbers in the national population, earlier retirement, increased affluence, and more social legitimation of their participation in leisure-oriented lifestyles.

Adapted with permission from "Interpretation for the Elderly: A Study of the Interpretive Interests of Retired National Parkgoers," by Gordon Bultena, Donald R. Field, and Renee Renninger. *Journal of Interpretation* 3:2 (1978): 29-32.

Study Design

Information was obtained in this study from behavioral observations of, and interviews with, older persons (aged 60 and older) visiting Olympic, Rainier, and North Cascades National Parks. A sampling design was employed whereby sites in each park were visited repeatedly in 1975. Data were obtained on older persons' attitudes and behaviors germane to their participation in organized interpretive programs (i.e., nature walks, talks, demonstrations, campfires). A total of 105 interpretive programs in the three parks were observed for purposes of obtaining information on the behavior of older participants. Opinions about these programs were solicited through informal interviews with participants.

Interviews also were conducted with 100 older persons in park campgrounds to elicit their observations and feelings about ongoing interpretive programs and to identify their interests and personal needs for interpretation. This camper population was felt to comprise a viable audience for park interpretive efforts, but it appeared to us that many older campers were not availing themselves of existing interpretive opportunities. Interview data were not collected from older visitors using local accommodations or from day users, except as they were contacted while participating in the formal interpretation programs.

Findings

Personal Characteristics

Retired parkgoers displayed several common charactertistics. Most were relatively young, recently retired, and despite problems with chronic disorders, saw themselves as being in good health. They led active lives and displayed very positive attitudes toward their present life situations. They were high spirited, adventurous, and desirous of acquiring more knowledge about the historical and natural features of the parks. All were strongly committed to conservationist goals and specifically to the necessity of preserving parklands for future generations. They diligently sought to obey park regulations and showed disdain for persons who would violate rules or engage in depreciative behaviors.

Most retired persons contacted in this study were visiting the national parks as couples, with or without other friends or family members. Widows, widowers, and singles were most often observed in multigenerational groups or peer groups in day use areas or in organized commercial tours. Although the most common group type was the senior couple, numerous two- and three-generational groups (comprised of grandchildren, children, siblings, younger friends, and age peers) were observed. Group composition was important to involvement of the aged in park interpretive programs, as is later discussed.

The activities of these older respondents, unlike many of the younger park visitors, were generally unhurried and open-ended. Although most had basic travel itineraries, they did not feel bound by these schedules and opted to stay in campgrounds until local sightseeing and recreational opportunities had been exhausted.

An important facet of campground culture was the frequent formation of friendship ties and helping patterns between age peers. Ephemeral social communities evolved as new parties arrived in the campgrounds and others departed. New arrivals typically were greeted by age peers and introduced around. Although striking differences in personality and degree of sociability were observed, retired persons consistently regarded each other with mutual trust, respect, and understanding. Reciprocal exchanges of information, services, and goods were common. In some instances, this took the form of assisting age peers on the park trails by carrying personal items or aiding their passage over difficult terrain. Nearly all respondents, however, were in sufficiently good health to navigate the self-guided walks and many sought out the more demanding front-country hiking trails.

Often the sightseeing activities and day trips of respondents were coordinated with those of newly found friends in the sharing of transportation. In some instances, new friendships were apparently maintained beyond the park setting, as visitors integrated their future travel plans and/or arranged home visits. A further finding was that many of the aged were involved in larger social networks that provided them up-to-date information on highway conditions, places to eat, things to see, and desirable places to camp. One result of this "grapevine" is that many older visitors became well informed about the content of interpretive programs, and even the names of the best naturalists, prior to their arrivals in the parks.

Attitudes Toward Interpretive Programs

Observations of daytime interpretive programs (fixed displays, talks, and nature walks) revealed that older persons regularly made up from 25 to 35 percent of the audiences. This figure jumped to about 65 percent at some popular sites. Interestingly, the representation of older persons in these programs was consistently underestimated by park managers, suggesting that the numerical prominence of this user group is not correctly perceived by officials.

While most of the respondents rated their participation in interpretive programs as enjoyable, many also expressed concern that the program formats were not effectively meeting their needs. A common criticism was that programs were primarily geared to first-time visitors and often were superficial and uninformative. Because of longer stays and more extensive parkgoing experience than many younger persons, some older visitors were already familiar with current interpretive content. Also, given their strong environmental commitments and prior knowledge of park flora and fauna, many sought more in-depth, challenging presentations than they felt were being provided.

The experiences of older persons on nature walks suggested some additional problems. First, older persons sometimes were left behind, especially on elevated trails, as interpreters and younger visitors rapidly proceeded from one observation site to the next. Interpreters usually appeared oblivious to this problem. It was not uncommon for older persons, just catching up, to find that the formal remarks had been concluded and the group was prepared to move on. Older persons also tended to be shuffled to the fringes of their groups as younger, often more aggressive, members sought access to park naturalists. Older persons sometimes experienced difficulties hearing in these situations and in gaining the attention of interpreters to ask questions.

A second complaint was that groups tended to be too large for sustained wildlife observation and for personal interaction with naturalists. Finally, groups sometimes were seen as affording too little opportunity for members to interact between themselves. The respondents saw opportunities for comraderie with other visitors as a particularly desirable, but often unrealized, by-product of their participation in formal interpretive programs.

Evening slide presentations and campfire programs held mixed appeal for older campers. Some felt that the information presented was superficial and redundant; some resented disruptions of young children and/or felt the programs conflicted with their activity schedules. For instance, it was not uncommon for respondents to be early risers and to retire early, or to devote evening hours to interaction with friends or the pursuit of hobbies or camp maintenance.

The composition of travel parties was important in the decisions of older persons to participate in evening programs. When grandchildren were present, retirees took considerable satisfaction in escorting them to evening programs and in sharing their excitement with a new activity. In fact, retirees were found to devote considerable time and effort to acquainting their grandchildren with camping and outdoor craft skills. In the absence of grandchildren, the evening interpretation programs held less attraction for respondents, although they were frequently reviewed as a vehicle for becoming acquainted with other campers.

Summary and Conclusions

Several conclusions about the efficacy of interpretive efforts for retirees are suggested by this study. Although observations were limited to three national parks in the Pacific Northwest, it is likely that the findings have relevance for interpretive programs in other parks as well. It was revealed that:

1. The prevalence of older persons in daytime interpretive programs was considerable, but their numbers were regularly underestimated by park officials.

2. Existing program efforts, while often positively evaluated by respondents, were not fully congruent with their felt needs. Often retirees were already familiar with the information being presented. Also, because their visits were

generally longer than those of younger people, many older persons had exhausted the range of interpretive offerings in the local area.

3. Retirees' special needs on nature walks often went unobserved by interpreters, and they informally expressed dissatisfaction with this activity. The large size and rigid pace of interpretive groups were points of particular concern.

4. An important motive for older persons participating in interpretive programs was the opportunity for interaction with others, especially age peers. Yet the formal, structured format of many programs seldom provided the time or opportunity for much interpersonal contact.

5. The content and scheduling of evening programs often precluded active participation by older persons, for several reasons.

Interpretation for the Aged

Given the numerical prominence of older persons among national park visitors, it appears that their special needs and interests should be more systematically solicited and carefully considered in planning interpretive efforts. Several suggestions follow with regard to possible directions of interpretive programming for this age group.

First, the image that park interpreters have of older visitors should be surveyed. There are many stereotypes about older persons that, if adopted by interpreters, could produce improper programming for this user group. Inservice educational programs may be required to sensitize park personnel to the characteristics, felt needs, and interpretive orientations of older visitors.

Second, consideration might be given to providing age-graded programs designed exclusively for older persons, as is now sometimes done with children. These programs could effectively speak both to the unique information needs of older visitors and could also be designed to facilitate opportunities for the desired social interaction with age peers. Age-graded programs also would remove a frequent irritant of age-integrated programs—disruptions by young children.

Third, new, in-depth interpretive presentations should be prepared for repeat visitors, who often have considerable knowledge about park history and natural ecosystems. In some cases, these presentations could be keyed to written materials that might be available on loan in the parks.

Fourth, comprehension of interpretive materials by the older population might be enhanced by more reference to aging processes and life-cycle patterns in nature (e.g., geological time, forest succession, lake eutrophication). The use of aging as a focal point for presentations would assist audience comprehension of the materials and better sensitize older visitors to the fact that life-cycle patterns are as much a part of natural ecosystems as they are of social systems and human life.

Fifth, the older visitor represents a virtually untapped resource for interpretive programming. Some persons probably have made visits to the park in its formative years, have had unusual park experiences, or have insights into park history that could be shared with newcomers. Perhaps "oldtimer programs" could be periodically scheduled at which audiences would be encouraged to reminisce and share experiences about their earlier visits to the parks.

Sixth, some older persons have hobbies (e.g., painting and photography) that might aid others' appreciation of park phenomena. One aged respondent, for example, was found to have an extensive set of slides on local birds that had been photographed in their natural habitat. The photographer, a self-educated ornithologist, had presented numerous programs on birds to groups in his home community. Special interpretive programs or craft fairs could be held at which hobbies could be displayed. In some instances, older visitors might be encouraged to participate in special living history programs in the parks.

Finally, greater use might be made of roving rangers to meet the interpretive needs of older visitors. These rangers could partly utilize the social networks that form among retirees to gain access to this population. By deliberately seeking out retirees, interpreters not only would be able to better ascertain their special interests and needs, but also to identify the personal skills and resources that they might bring to broader and more dynamic interpretive programming in the parks.

A Sociological Look
At the Japanese Tourist

Gary E. Machlis
Donald R. Field
Mark E. Van Every

Introduction

IN THE PAST decade, the United States has increasingly become a destination for international tourists. Technological achievements such as wide-bodied jet aircraft, improved economic equality between the world's industrial populations, and reduction of governmental travel barriers have contributed to this increase. Americans, who in the 1950s and 60s toured the world in large numbers and often controversial style, are now finding themselves hosts to people from other lands. This shift in travel patterns among the world's citizenry is not without its consequences for outdoor recreation places in the United States. Parks, forests, and historic sites once used predominantly by American citizens are now being visited by foreign tourists. These travelers add a unique element to the growing diversity of user populations. For the interpreter, they signal a new "need to know," as the successful planning and conduct of interpretive programs may now require an understanding of visitor publics widely different from traditional users.

This paper focuses on Japanese tourists. Japan represents the third largest source of foreign visitors to the United States (after

Adapted from "Foreign Visitors and Interpretation: A Sociological Look at the Japanese Tourist," by Gary E. Machlis, Donald R. Field, and Mark E. Van Every. (Paper presented at the Northwest Association of Interpretive Naturalists, Seattle, Washington, October 14-16, 1981).

Canada and Mexico), and the U.S.A. is the most popular travel destination for the Japanese (U.S. Dept. of Commerce 1972). Hence, Japan represents a potentially important source of foreign visitors to U.S. parks and historic sites. Further, Japan is the only non-Western industrialized society; its cultural base is much different than other tourist-exporting nations. The purpose of this paper is to 1) provide information about Japanese travelers, the Japanese tourism industry, and Japanese society, and 2) to suggest how such information can directly aid interpretive programming.

A sociological profile of visitors is a first step in such an effort, for it can outline the "natural history" and behavioral patterns of diverse publics that frequent outdoor recreation sites. Several variables seem important. Machlis *et al.* write:

> When visitors enter a park, they reflect certain *sociodemographic characteristics* such as age and family life cycles, and these factors may influence participation. Visitors depend upon a set of *human institutions* to help organize their recreation experiences—transportation systems, tour operators, travel agents, clubs, associations and so forth. Finally, they rely upon *key cultural elements* to guide their individual action. Examples would include ethical systems, attitudes toward Nature, and norms for proper conduct (1981:201).

Our description of Japanese tourists is organized around these three variables: sociodemographic characteristics, human institutions, and key cultural elements.

Methods

There is no paucity of general tourism statistics. Dwyer *et al.* (1979) list twenty-two major U.S. organizations collecting tourism data, and this does not include many state, private, and site-specific efforts. Abundant aggregate information is available about the characteristics of tourists, destinations and origins, reasons for travel, methods of transportation, travel expenditures, and so forth. However, few studies provide specific information on interpretation-related activities.

While we could not locate specific studies dealing with Japanese tourism to U.S. parks and historic sites, several statistical reports can provide an overview of Japanese tourism to the United

States. The first is *Tourism in Japan* (1979, 1981) published by the Japanese National Tourist Organization (JNTO). The second is a survey conducted by the U.S. Travel Service (1978), which reports 1977 data for 2,533 surveyed Japanese travelers. A third source is a similar study conducted by the U.S. Department of Commerce (USDC) (1972). Several works provided qualitative information on Japanese society (Reischauer 1978; Nakane 1970; Vogel 1963) and the role of leisure in Japan (Lebra 1976; Linhart 1975).

Sociodemographic Characteristics

General Visitation Patterns

Japan's rise as a major industrial power has resulted in a steady increase in the number of Japanese traveling abroad. In 1967 there were 267,538 overseas travelers; by 1979 there were over 4 million (Table 1). Tourism is a major factor, as 83.6 percent of all 1977 travelers were involved in pleasure activities (JNTO 1979).

Table 1. Number of Japanese traveling abroad

Year	Number of travelers	Percentage change over previous year
1967	267,538	+ 26.0
1968	343,542	+ 28.4
1969	492,880	+ 43.6
1970	663,467	+ 34.6
1971	961,135	+ 44.9
1972	1,392,045	+ 44.8
1973	2,288,966	+ 64.4
1974	2,335,530	+ 2.0
1975	2,466,326	+ 5.6
1976	2,852,584	+ 5.7
1977	3,151,431	+ 10.5
1978	3,525,110	+ 11.9
1979	4,038,298	+ 14.6

Source: Immigration Bureau, Ministry of Justice (JNTO 1979, 1981).

The United States is the major destination of Japanese overseas visitors. Within the United States, Japanese vacation travelers are concentrated within the Pacific Rim (Guam, Hawaii, and the Far West), though a sizeable portion visit the East Coast. Table 2 shows that while 72 percent of all Japanese travelers surveyed

Table 2.   United States destinations of 1977 Japanese travelers

U.S.A. destination visited	Percentage of travelers surveyed[1] (N = 1,096)
Mainland	51
New England	4
Eastern Gateway	19
George Washington Country	6
The South	6
Great Lakes Country	7
Mountain West	3
Frontier West	8
Far West	47
U. S. Islands	72
Guam	11
Hawaii	61

Source: U.S. Travel Service (1978).
[1] Percentages do not add to 100, since many travelers visited more than one destination.

Table 3.   Activities Japanese travelers would be interested in undertaking on a trip to the mainland

Interesting activities	Percentage of travelers surveyed
Experience the scenery	44
Visit several cities	41
Visit historical places	34
See the "wild west"	32
Make purchases	31
Take a restful vacation	24
Enjoy the nightlife	22
Visit museums	22
Visit national parks	22
Gamble	21
Get to know the American people	21
Visit the Rocky Mountains	20
Spend time on beaches	18
Go skiing	9
Go to sports events	9

Source: USDC (1972).

visited U.S. islands, less than 5 percent visited the Mountain West or New England regions. Hence, it is the western national parks and eastern historical areas that are likely to have the largest numbers of Japanese visitors.

A study conducted by Japan Air Lines (cited in USDC 1972) suggests that national parks are important locales for Japanese tourists. When asked what activities they would be interested in undertaking on a trip to the mainland, visiting national parks was mentioned by 22 percent of all travelers (Table 3). Several alternatives (experience the scenery, visit historical places, visit museums, and so forth) are likely to involve interpretation as well, hence 22 percent is a conservative estimate of the proportion of Japanese visitors interested in interpretation-related activities.

Awareness of specific national parks is surprisingly high among Japanese international travelers, and their relative interest (the percentage of those aware of a place that are interested in visiting it) is also quite strong. Table 4 shows that while Niagara Falls and Disneyland rate highest in awareness (89 percent), Grand Canyon generates the highest relative interest (63 percent).

Table 4.   Awareness of and interest in specific attractions among Japanese travelers, 1972

Attractions	Heard of (percentage)	Interested in visiting (percentage)	Relative[1] interest (percentage)
Niagara Falls	89	53	60
Disneyland	89	39	44
Statue of Liberty	86	28	33
Rocky Mountains	84	30	36
Cape Kennedy	80	25	31
Grand Canyon	70	44	63
New England	56	14	25
Yellowstone National Park	41	17	41
Banff National Park	20	11	55
Everglades National Park	16	5	31

Source: USDC (1972).
[1] Computed only among those aware of each attraction.

Demographic Characteristics

The Japanese traveler to the United States tends to be a young adult male with at least some college education. Yet, as Table 5 shows, travel to the United States is not restricted to an elite, highly educated class. Most visitors, 58 percent, are in the 18-34 age group, and the median age is 30 (U.S. Travel Service 1978). Since the Japanese often combine business and pleasure trips, reliable figures will include business travelers. In 1979, visas for pleasure accounted for about 84 percent of the visitors, while business visas encompasses about 12 percent (Bolyard 1981). Even so, 39 percent of all 1977 travelers had less than a college education, and 50 percent were clerical workers, students, unemployed, or retired. These numbers vary greatly according to destination: a high proportion of males visit the frontier West; educational levels are higher among mainland visitors.

Table 5.   Characteristics of Japanese travelers to the U.S.A.

Traveler characteristics	Percentage of Total Travelers to U.S.A. (N = 1,096)
Sex	
Male	56
Female	44
Education	
Elementary/Primary	5
High School	34
Technical/Jr. College	17
College/Post Graduate	45
Occupation	
Professional/Executive	20
Clerical	27
Student	11
Sales	9
Self-employed	17
Unemployed/Retired	12
Other	5

Source: U.S. Travel Service (1978).

While 58 percent of total travelers claim to speak or read English, Reischauer (1978) suggests that fluency is much lower, due to the methods of English training used in Japanese schools. Vacation travelers claim the lowest English capability (49 percent), an important factor in interpretive planning for Japanese visitors.

Data on the kind of social units common to Japanese tourists is incomplete but suggests that the organized tour group is important. Table 6 illustrates that in 1972 and 1976 a large number of Japanese vacation travelers to the United States were involved in organized tours. In addition, over one-third of the visitors were in groups of four or more. However, the number of visitors involved in tours decreased from 1972 to 1976, while the number traveling alone or outside of tours has increased.

Table 6.   Characteristics of trip, Japanese visitors to U.S.A.

Characteristics	Percentage of Japanese visitors	
	1972	1976
Type of fare purchased		
First class	3	4
Regular economy/coach	22	32
Discount/excursion	18	18
Charter	3	4
Tour package	55	43
Inclusive tour travel		
Yes	71	65
No	29	35
Size of traveling party		
1 person	13	18
2 persons	39	36
3 persons	12	10
4 or more persons	35	36

Source: USDC (1972); U.S. Travel Service (1978).

Human Institutions

Travel in Japan

Japan is an island country, a modern economic power, and a rapidly changing but traditional society. The Japanese are curious about other people and have a history of travel. Off-island travel began with the dramatic voyages by priests and grandees to China and Korea; they were followed by the rich and intelligentsia until the closing of borders in 1936. During World War II, wartime visits and duty tours exposed many Japanese to other cultures. Currently, the young adults of Japan are traveling in increasing numbers.

Travel is becoming a status symbol in Japan for several reasons. As in most industrialized countries, manufactured goods are valued possessions in Japan. Lebra (1976) lists the "3 C's" as a consumptive goal: car, cooler (air conditioner), and color television; tourist travel competes with these other luxuries. The U.S. Department of Commerce (1972) suggests that travel has become a fourth consumptive goal for several reasons: Japanese ownership of manufactured goods is extremely high, cars are expensive relative to travel, and Japanese society provides for an extended youth before marriage. This population has time and money for touring.

Table 7.   Average household expenditures for leisure-related items[1]

	1975	1976	1977	1978	1979
Dining out	68.1	71.1	73.8	78.8	84.9
Culture and recreation	87.4	90.8	93.2	95.4	97.6
Travel	47.1	45.9	44.8	48.4	47.9
Total household expenditures	1,895.8	1,919.0	1,935.6	1,974.4	2,028.7
% of total household expenditures spent on leisure-related items	21.5	21.4	21.5	22.2	22.8

Source: JNTO (1981).
[1] All figures are in thousands of Yen, adjusted for buying power using 1975 as a base year.

Surprisingly, expenditures for travel remained fairly constant for 1975-1979 (Table 7). Only 2.3 percent of total household expenditures in 1979 were used for travel, while all leisure-related items accounted for 22.8 percent of the total.

Leisure in Japan

Japan is beginning to evolve work/non-work patterns common to industrialized societies: short stretches of off season, a traditional summer vacation, weekend free time, and a daily cycle managed by the industrial work clock. The five-day work week has been officially encouraged in Japan since 1973; in 1978, 44.7 percent of all firms had adopted the system (JNTO 1981). However, strong occupational differences are still present. The professional and salaryman (manager) have nonwork cycles amenable to tourism; the businessman may travel for business and recreational reasons at the same time. Leisure cycles in Japan are in a state of flux (Vogel 1963).

Tourism must fit into these evolving cycles, and the Japanese system of holidays is expected to provide more time for longer trips. Excluding weekends, the average number of annual holidays is 16.5 days (JNTO 1981). Major holidays include New Year's Day, Golden Week (which begins on the Emperor's Birthday, April 29, and ends on Constitution Day, May 3), and Vernal Equinox Day (March 20), which is evolving into a long weekend (USDC 1972).

Countering this increase in leisure is the Japanese attitude toward time spent away from work. Several authors (Vogel 1963; Lebra 1976; Linhart 1975) suggest that the Japanese worker is

Table 8.   Leisure activities of the Japanese people

Activity	Daily leisure time (multiple answer) Percentage (N = 1,052)	Long-term leisure period (multiple answer) Percentage (N = 1,052)	Leisure activities desired (multiple answer) Percentage (N = 1,052)
Enjoy TV/radio	87.7 (1)	19.0 (2)	0.1
Read newspapers	76.5 (2)	8.1	0.1
Chat with family	49.6 (3)	7.4	1.0
Read books	49.2 (4)	9.9 (6)	3.3 (10)
Mix with friends, acquaintances or neighbors	35.1 (5)	6.1	1.7
Mix with relatives	26.7 (6)	11.8 (5)	1.2
Take a nap	24.2 (7)	8.0 (10)	1.6
Listen to records or taped music	23.5 (8)	6.3	2.1
Dine out or go shopping	22.1 (9)	12.5 (4)	1.4
Educate children	21.2 (10)	2.6	1.8
Go to a movie or watch sports	16.8	9.6 (7)	3.9 (8)
Participate in sports	13.0	9.5 (8)	8.8 (3)
Take a drive	6.9	8.6 (9)	1.8
Take a day trip or day hike	10.8	17.8 (3)	5.7 (6)
Take an overnight or longer trip in Japan	10.6	43.3 (1)	24.6 (2)
Enjoy handicrafts, horticulture or collecting stamps	19.3	5.3	3.9 (8)
Engage in artistic activities	12.3	4.2	5.2 (7)
Study to acquire qualifications or techniques	6.8	1.9	8.7 (4)
Learn to perform tea ceremony/flower arrangements, cook, or sew	8.5	1.9	8.2 (5)
Travel abroad	0.6	2.7	25.7 (1)

Note: The numbers in ( ) denote rankings.
Source: A survey conducted by the Better Living Information Center, 1975, cited in JNTO (1979).

prevented by custom and obligation from taking days off which he or she has accrued. In 1969, 40 percent of Japanese employees used less than half of their allotted holidays with differences in this figure according to sex, age, and occupation (Linhart 1975). Only two strata in Japanese society have the full right to enjoy their leisure— youth (not part of the production process) and the elderly (retired from active work).

Further, traditional Japanese forms of leisure seem incompatible with the aggressive activity of the modern tourist. Linhart (1975) suggests that Japanese leisure is more passive than active, and that this orientation has been slow to change. Table 8 profiles

1975 leisure activities of the Japanese people. The most popular pursuits include reading books, enjoying TV and radio, and talking with family members. Significantly, travel abroad, participated in by only 2.7 percent of respondents over a long-term period, was the most desired activity mentioned (25.7 percent).

Yet a description of Japanese leisure activities by Reischauer provides a different picture:

> Japan is a land of mass spectator sports and mass activities . . . Ski slopes are hazardously crowded in winter. The Shonan beaches near Tokyo will attract over a million persons on a hot summer weekend. An endless antlike chain of people on the slopes of Mt. Fuji turn mountain climbing in summer into a mass sport. Sightseeing crowds, mostly organized groups of school children and village and town associations, inundate famous beauty spots in the spring and autumn sightseeing seasons and all but obliterate them from view or even existence (1978:202).

Hence, Japanese attitudes toward vacations, tourism, outdoor recreation and travel abroad seem somewhat unclear.

The Tourist Industry in Japan

The tourist industry in Japan is highly dynamic, expanding rapidly, and developing a tie to Japan's basic economic structure (USDC 1972). Japanese attachment and dependency upon employers is widely acknowledged; what company one works for is more basic to one's identification than what one does (Lebra 1976). Vogel notes:

> In Japan, the basic mode of integration into the economic order is not through occupational specialty, but through the firm (1963:264).

The Japanese worker is likely to travel in groups either organized by his or her firm or in groups of similar workers. This close relationship of work and play has resulted in the centralization of the Japanese tourist industry. Most big industrial firms have their own travel agencies, and in 1972 six major producers accounted for 50 percent of wholesale travel activity (USDC 1972).

There are at least four major kinds of managed tours in Japan, excluding independent travel arranged by a travel agent. *Package tours* are fully managed tours, where all arrangements and many activities are organized by the agent. The group size is often quite large (as high as 300 persons). The proportion of Japanese travelers using package tours varies by destination; it is high for Guam (79.9 percent) and Hawaii (53.8 percent), while lower for the U.S. mainland. For young travelers, package tours provide low bulk fares; for older tourists there is the security of a preplanned trip.

Affinity Groups are tours organized by firms, industries, and cooperatives, where members either know each other or have an occupational relationship. For example, the Association of Agricultural Cooperatives has its own travel agency, with an annual production of 10,000 tour passengers (USDC 1972). Farmers participate in tours of special agricultural interest, visiting attractions such as the produce terminal in San Francisco or the Farmer's Market in Seattle and Los Angeles. Affinity groups vary in size.

Special Study tours are a kind of affinity group, but with an even more occupational oriented framework. These tours are intense programs of travel, geared to learning new methods, viewing industrial sites, and conducting trade interviews. These groups usually have between ten and forty people. There is some resistance to these trips in the United States. USDC (1972) reports that Japanese travel agents report a growing reluctance among U.S. manufacturers to receive such tour groups for plant visits.

Incentive Travel tours are benefits provided by employers to workers, either through outright grant, low-cost loan, or company-managed saving program. Workers have a wide variety of choices, and travel agencies may include these tourists in their package tours. Group size varies but is usually over forty-five, in order to take advantage of bulk air fares.

Key Cultural Elements

Japanese tourists bring a variety of social norms with them on trips to the United States. These norms, derived in part from key elements of Japanese culture, can serve as guides to Japanese tourist behavior. However, such norms are surely not ironclad. Reischauer notes:

> Though a homogeneous people culturally, the roughly 115 million Japanese display great variation of attitudes and ways of life by age

group and according to their diverse roles in society. A teenager and an octogenerian, a day laborer and a corporation executive, a bank clerk and an artist show about as much diversity in attitudes as their counterparts would in any Western country. Almost anything that might be said about Japanese in general would not be true of many and might be flatly contradicted by some (1978:124).

Four elements are discussed: belongingness, empathy, dependency, and occupying the proper place (Lebra 1976).

Belongingness

Japan is a social society. What would strictly be a private matter in an individualistic culture tends to be a group enterprise in Japan. We have mentioned that the Japanese white collar worker's recreation is often organized by his or her employer (Linhart 1975). The Japanese individual feels more comfortable in a group than alone, and it is not surprising that Japanese tourists prefer group tours to individualized travel (USDC 1972).

This sense of belongingness begins well before an expected trip or vacation. Travel begins with a "separation party," where friends and relatives wish the tourist well and offer gifts. An obligation to return the gifts is accepted, and Japanese tourists often spend considerable vacation time making these purchases. Table 9 shows that 21 percent of tour travelers' expenditures are for purchases; the number is lower (13 percent) for individual travelers.

Table 9.   Distribution of expenditures by Japanese travelers, as percentages of all expenditures, 1972

Activity	Tour travelers		Individual travelers	
	Pacific area	Intercontinental	Pacific area	Intercontinental
Tour price/primary transportation	53	61	39	52
Local transportation	2	4	5	6
Lodging[1]	1	2	14	12
Food/drink	2	5	10	10
Purchases	32	21	21	13
Miscellany/sightseeing	9	7	11	7

Source: USDC (1972).
[1] Outside the framework of the tour.

Empathy

Empathy rates high among Japanese virtues. In a group-oriented culture such as Japan, decision making often requires consensus, and confrontation tends to be avoided. Nonverbal communication is highly valued and widely practiced and, in such a homogeneous country, applicable to many social situations. Reischauer describes the general process:

> Varying positions are not sharply outlined and their differences analyzed and clarified. Instead, each participant in a discussion feels his way cautiously, only unfolding his own views as he sees how others react to them. Much is suggested by indirection or vague implication. Thus, any sharp conflict of views is avoided before it comes into the open. The Japanese even have a word, *haragei*, "the art of the belly," for this meeting of minds, or at least the viscera, without clear verbal interaction (1978:148).

Conversations are punctuated with agreements and gestures of approval; to the Japanese, an American host may seem not to be listening because of his or her silence while a Japanese guest is speaking.

Dependency

Much has been written about the dependency of Japanese children upon their mothers, and the impact of this relationship on Japanese society (Vogel 1963; Lebra 1976). Other dependent relations exist; the employer-employee relationship is likewise based on dependency and service. This conflicts with American ideas of autonomy and individual equality. Many Japanese tourists to the United States are often put off by the self-service operations of American tourist sites; others find freedom with their lack of involvement in dependency relations.

Occupying the Proper Place

The Japanese are sensitive to rank order (i.e., "occupying the proper place"). Japanese language, social customs and values are all organized to illustrate the rank order of interacting individuals. When Japanese tourists visit countries with egalitarian ideologies (like the United States), the host/guest relationship may be influenced by this limitation. Lebra writes:

The cultural dearth of ways to express horizontal or status-neutral relationships forces the actor to make a binary choice between respectful, formal behavior and disrespectful, informal behavior (1976:53).

Japanese tourists may express "disdain" toward "backward" peoples, including Asian neighbors. Lebra (1976) makes note of the rude behavior exhibited by Japanese tourists in Southeast Asia. For tourists in the national parks, slight gradations in occupation may signal rank order, and it is a common custom of Japanese tourists to address a host by his occupation (Mr. Park Ranger, Ms. Travel Agent, etc.).

Applying the Information to Interpretation

How can such information aid interpretive efforts? We would suggest that better understanding of Japanese tourists would be useful in 1) visitor management, 2) information services, 3) the planning of interpretive programs, and 4) the conduct of interpretive programs.

Visitor Management

Visitor management can be crucial to effective interpretation. The high percentage of Japanese tourists who travel in tour groups (Table 7) represents an obvious opportunity; the cooperation of tour organizers can help dispense visitors to less crowded areas, can help promote safety, and can allow park interpretive staff to plan ahead. The centralization of the tourist industry in Japan suggests that contact with major wholesalers might allow the forecasting of future trends in Japanese visitation. Another suggestion would be to develop a "travel wholesaler's planning guide" to popular parks and historic areas. Such a guide could aid in development of the travel itineraries, bookings, and brochures used in Japan and could further coordinate the flow of tour groups and interpretive programming.

The data on travel expenditures (Table 9) suggest that "trophy-taking" (buying postcards, souvenir shopping, and so forth) are major components of the Japanese tourist's park experience. Hence, concessionaires and historical associations may need to be included in planning for Japanese visitors.

Information Services

The fact that the Japanese tourist is unlikely to be fluent in English, or to have had much experience in U.S. National Parks, makes the provision of basic information extremely important. All visitors require information concerning shelter, food, medical attention, regulations, and so forth. To serve the Japanese tourist, several alternatives exist: the necessary information can be translated into Japanese, presented in English with ideograms, or a translator can be made available. Parks with growing Japanese visitation should have access to a translator, in case of emergency.

For more detailed information (such as the natural history of an area), arrangements can be made with nearby universities and language institutes to translate key publications. These translations can be handed out along with English versions of park guides and materials. An often overlooked approach is to purchase a small quantity of relevant Japanese reading materials from overseas publishers. In any event, many Japanese *are* fluent in English, and often tour group leaders can aid interpreters in communication.

The high awareness and relative interest in national parks shown by Japanese tourists reflects the use of parks as attractions in tourism advertising. Travel posters extolling the pleasures of an American vacation often include pictures of Grand Canyon, New York Gateway, Niagara Falls, and so forth. It is unclear, however, what information is actually communicated to potential visitors. Efforts to provide Japanese tourist organizations (such as JNTO) with up-to-date, accurate, and relevant information could result in increased visitation, greater cooperation by tour groups, and higher satisfaction of tourist's expectations.

Planning Interpretive Programs

Our profile of Japanese tourists presents several problems to the interpreter interested in "connecting" with foreign visitors. First, Table 8 suggests a passive orientation to Japanese leisure, and interpretation-related activities (such as visiting an art museum or zoo) rate somewhat low. However, Reischauer's description of Japanese outdoor recreation, and the high participation in day trips and hikes (17.8 percent over a long-term period), indicates an active, outdoor-oriented leisure. Wise interpretive planning might include both active and passive exhibits, opportunities for both quiet contemplation and participation in group activities.

A second problem is the combination of high education (Table 5), and a strong language barrier. Merely simplifying introductory material is often not appropriate. Translations of introductory material may be inadequate for Japanese tourists interested in natural or social history. A clear solution, whenever possible, would be to supply tour groups with material before an interpretive program, and to use the tour leader (often fluent in English) as an interpreter.

We have described several kinds of Japanese tour groups and suggested that participants often have an employer, occupation, or interest in common. Knowing ahead of time the kind of tour group to visit a site can be of great benefit to the interpreter, and he or she may use this information in choosing a subject, selecting a medium, and organizing a program. The difficulty lies in developing a link with the wholesale travel agents, and in the fact that 35 percent of Japanese tourists to the U.S. in 1976 did not prepurchase tour activities (Table 7).

Conducting Interpretive Programs

The conduct of interpretive programs for Japanese tourists may require special forethought. Japanese tour groups of fifty or more people are common, and such large audiences may be unworkable for programs that demand quiet, have limited staff, or are held in small spaces. Yet, other kinds of programs (campfires, movies, self-guided trailwalks) *are* amenable to bigger groups and should be satisfactory. Analyses by Reischauer (1978) and Lebra (1976) suggest that Japanese are generally group-oriented and have much experience in group activities. It may be more difficult to engage tour group participants in individual involvement, such as handling an antique reproduction, expressing an opinion on park facilites, or deviating from the group itinerary.

Besides a group orientation, several key elements of Japanese culture are of importance to the interpreter. Japanese manners consider quick individual decision making impolite, and the interpreter who is dependent upon immediate audience feedback may be disappointed. A traditional respect for rank may be misunderstood as insincere deference to uniformed personnel. The obligation of the traveler to return to Japan with gifts obviously requires large amounts of time spent shopping, rather than attending interpretive programs. Most importantly, almost all available data point to the high motivation of Japanese travelers for learning about other environments and cultures. Table 3 showed that 44 percent of Japanese travelers are interested in "experiencing the scenery"; Table 4 illustrated the high relative interest in visiting national parks; Table 8 showed the general Japanese interest in travel abroad. Hence, Japanese visitors to national parks may be quite eager to benefit from interpretation.

Conclusion

This paper has taken a sociological look at Japanese tourists and has tried to outline the sociodemographic characteristics, human institutions, and key cultural elements that help shape their participation at interpretation-related recreation sites. Elsewhere we have written:

> Simple as it may sound, the matching of an interpretive approach
> with the appropriate audience is perhaps the most difficult challenge
> facing those responsible for the array of public contact programs
> now offered by the National Park Service and equivalent preserves
> (Machlis and Field 1974:19).

As the number of foreign visitors to parks increases, this job becomes more difficult and challenging. Interpretation for foreign visitors has a special urgency: it offers an opportunity for cross-cultural and world understanding.

Cruise Ship Travelers to Alaska

Barbara A. Koth
Donald R. Field
Roger N. Clark

Introduction

CRUISE SHIPS EMERGED as a major form of recreation travel in Southeast Alaska in the 1950s, but their popularity soared in the 1970s. In 1979, 70,000 passengers visited Alaska via this mode of travel to national park and forest lands bordering aquatic resource systems. The purpose of this article is to describe this leisure experience and to identify interpretive alternatives appropriate to each phase of the social event. It is not our purpose to introduce new or novel interpretive techniques, and some of the methods discussed actually are in current use on Alaskan cruise ships. Instead, this chapter suggests that the interpretive audience can be reached more effectively by coordinating and matching message content and method with trip phase.

The cruise ship as a leisure setting offers unique opportunities for interpreters to interact with a recreational public over an extended period of time, rather than during a single event. The long-term nature of this leisure experience allows presentation of interpretive material in phases appropriate to the level of interest and accumulated knowledge of passengers. A "building block" approach is possible, where material delivered to the audience at later stages is contingent upon earlier presentations and knowledge achieved by the message recipients. Details are added to the

Adapted with permission from "Cruise Ship Travelers to Alaska: Implications for Onboard Interpretation," by Barbara A. Koth, Donald R. Field, and Roger N. Clark. *The Interpreter* 13:1 (Winter 1981): 39-46.

background initially provided. At the conclusion of such a trip, passengers would possess a complete set of information.

Additionally, the cruise ship offers opportunities for using a variety of techniques and topics to effectively deliver the interpretive message. Travel to Southeast Alaska has the potential for integrating the five types of tourism outlined by Smith (1977). *Ethnic, cultural,* and *historic* tourism, respectively, focus attention on Tlingit and Haida native lifestyle as a function of occupation and transportation networks on past Russian influence, and on native/white interaction. While the *environment* (scenery and wildlife) provides a backdrop for observing these human factors, *recreational* tourism is the lure onboard, as passengers participate in various play activities and scheduled entertainment events. Whereas the majority of other vacation locations can be defined by fewer factors, in this cruise ship situation all five elements provide the impetus for travel; this calls for unusually diverse interpretive programs.

Background

The cruise ship industry in Southeast Alaska is very regular in terms of visitation. Six companies and nine ships operated during the 1979 season, and round-trip visits ranging from 7 to 14 days in duration departed from Los Angeles, San Francisco and Vancouver, B.C. The majority of ships visit the southeastern locales in the following sequence: Ketchikan, Juneau, Skagway, Glacier Bay and Sitka. One-way travel on the ships can occur as passengers connect at transfer points (Skagway, Juneau) with commercial tours to the Interior and Yukon. After completing these itineraries travelers can return home via aircraft, coach, or cruise ship.

At present, numerous onboard events are scheduled with emphasis on entertainment; only occasional information programs relate to Southeast Alaska. The use of educational material varies dramatically from ship to ship, ranging from a proliferation of movies, slide programs, public address systems,and personal talks to a complete lack of any interpretive offerings. At Glacier Bay National Monument, National Park Service rangers come aboard for the day to describe the glacial environment.

Methodology

Webb *et al.* (1966) argue for use of supplemental research methods (e.g., participant observation and other unobtrusive measures) in addition to reliance on the traditionally employed questionnaire. By joint use of survey and observation methods, it is possible to minimize biases and define areas of consensus in the findings from each method. Observation provides firsthand information on the interrelationships between activities, participants, and meanings within a leisure setting.

During the summer of 1979, researchers sailed on three round-trip, seven-day cruises and made informal observations to determine the nature of social interaction during the cruise. Impressions gathered through those informal observations form the basis of this chapter. Observers focused on the combination of spatial, temporal, and behavioral variables and their relationship to information flow. Spatial elements were identified by mapping the dominant use of facility areas by passengers. Temporal variations in activity patterns by time of day and length of cruise were recorded, and behavior and the development of social networks were noted as they influenced informal information transfer. A field journal, informal interviews, and directed conversation formed the basis for subsequent analysis. Federal personnel associated with provision of interpretive services, cruise directors, crew members, and travel agents wre utilized as informants to cross-reference observed patterns.

Phases of Cruise Experience

The cruise ship experience is here categorized into five phases based on observations of travelers' activity patterns, relationship to the Alaska environment, and social contacts during the trip. The development of the cruise as a social event includes several stages: 1) planning and anticipation of the trip and travel to departure port, 2) embarkation, 3) early sailing northbound, 4) visiting ports and Glacier Bay, and 5) traveling toward home port. This phasing is similar to the stages of a recreational experience defined by Clawson and Knetsch (1966): anticipation of event, travel to the site, the on-site experience, travel from the recreational setting, and recollection. Our analytical phases for cruise ship travel to Alaska and their relationship to the Clawson and Knetsch's typology are presented in Table 1.

Table 1.   Comparison of Phases of Recreation Experience

Alaska Cruise Ship	Clawson and Knetsch
1) planning and anticipation of trip and travel to departure	— anticipation of event — travel to the site
2) embarkation	
3) early sailing northbound	— on-site experience
4) visiting ports and Glacier Bay	
5) traveling toward home port recollection at home	— travel from the site — recollection

Planning, Anticipation, and Travel to Departure Port

The planning and anticipation phase includes pretrip activities from preliminary information gathering to packing and leaving home. The time lag between confirmation of reservations and departure may exceed one year for some individuals. Steamship companies provide introductory information regarding shipboard matters, payment, embarkation location, and itinerary material during this period.

Passengers can take a variety of modes of transportation for travel to the departure port. "Block booking," where travel companies reserve a block of accommodations for many clients departing from the same geographical region is common. Travel agents book passengers on the cruise ship who have not met previously but share similar itineraries on chartered flights or buses to the port of embarkation. Upon arrival, check-in procedures at the pier complex require standing in line and waiting in public areas prior to boarding.

Embarkation

Upon embarkation there is an extravagant welcome by ship officers, a proliferation of complimentary drinks, much picture taking, and incessant attention from employees. During boarding, passengers begin to learn the informal rules by which shipboard behavior is governed, and one of these norms allows for unlimited passenger communication. This is achieved in part by creation of an atmosphere of luxury where details of ship arrangements are handled by company personnel and the passenger is free to meet new acquaintances. Travelers perceive commonalities with others onboard due to this treatment, and communication channels remain open throughout the duration of the cruise.

Early Sailing Northbound

The early sailing northbound is characterized by a familiarization process, including discovery of ship facilities, introduction to traveling companions, and a desire for information providing an overview of natural and cultural aspects of the trip. The ship is passing along the largely undeveloped coastline of British Columbia, and observation of scenery and sighting of marine mammals are popular activities during this phase. Reinforcement of group social bonds is primarily facilitated by the scheduled events taking place daily. Activities on the first portion of the cruise are of an introductory nature, familiarizing passengers with each other, the crew, and ship facilities. These include a Welcome Aboard/Get Together Party, the Captain's Dinner, a singles' party, lessons for the games played in the casino, and various team games of a humorous nature. Ongoing entertainment events are numerous and include, for example, nightly dancing and music, costume contests and games, and instructional classes. These offerings vary from ship to ship, but there is a constant variety of simultaneous offerings.

Visiting Ports

Upon reaching Alaskan waters, the schedule changes to alternate onboard and shore activities as port visitation occurs. Several hours are spent in the port of call, with the majority of passengers taking a short bus tour providing an overview of local culture, history and environment. While shore time is limited, it is possible for passengers to participate in other self-initiated activities (e.g., shopping, walking tour) in the remaining time allotted. After reboarding, passengers participate in scheduled evening events. All travel, with the exception of cruising in Glacier Bay, is within Tongass National Forest. At Glacier Bay, National Park Service

naturalists provide reading material, present a formal program
outlining the park's natural and cultural history, and identify
locations of interest over the public address system. No stops are
made during this segment of the trip.

From our observations, it seems that intensity of interest in
attractions in ports decreases after visitation to the initial ports,
and little interaction with residents is noted during shore time.
Utilization of outdoor deck space when traveling between ports is
infrequent as compared with prior phases of the trip. Glacier Bay
represents the high point of the itinerary for round-trip passengers
and is the sole location during this phase where an interest in
scenery is observed. However, one-way passengers board during
port visitation, so behaviors specific to embarkation and early trip
phases are superimposed upon the predominant pattern.

Traveling Toward Home Port

While traveling to the home port, no stops are made en route.
Numerous shipboard events are scheduled, including those which
highlight trip activities and travels. Observation of scenery and
wildlife sighting cease to be important daily events during the later
stages of the trip, as do all factors associated with the outside
environment. Having seen a sampling of locations and events
which represent Alaska, focus shifts to entertainment and social
events. Upon disembarking many passengers interact with their
families and oncoming passengers.

Interpretation Alternatives

Planning and Anticipation and Travel to Departure Port

Pretrip expectations often shape the nature of tourists' impressions and post-trip satisfaction. For many passengers the cruise to
Alaska represents fulfillment of a long-term desire, and interpretive possibilities abound to fill the "at home" informational gap
when anticipation is high. Since many ships are booked to capacity one season in advance, the time between reservations and
departure is substantial. Material presented at this phase facilitates
planning for port and shipboard activities.

At this stage, passengers' communication is limited solely to correspondence with the company with which the cruise is booked, with traveling companions, and perhaps with prior visitors. Information provided during the anticipation phase could serve as a basis for entry into discussions upon boarding and help avoid future discontinuities and lowered satisfaction levels by creating realistic expectations.

Prior to embarkation, passengers might receive with ticket mailings pertinent weather and clothing information and addresses to write for additional information of interest (e.g., federal agencies and park units, chambers of commerce). Familiarity gained by reading relevant material appears to be a major source of satisfaction, and the provision of a bibliography could direct passengers to appropriate library sources.

Providing a pocket diary for keeping a social record of names and cabin members of new friends would aid in group formation. The diary also might be a means of dispersing relevant information, such as brief descriptions of major animal species that might be seen en route. The species described in each diary could vary, so that information exchanges would be encouraged. The social record could be provided at one of two key phases in the trip—trip planning or embarkation. Name tags and identification buttons for passengers (as provided by some tour companies) would allow for instant recognition while traveling.

Embarkation

During embarkation passengers focus on the ship and port of embarkation. Since this phase occurs rapidly and alternative activities are rigidly constrained by company procedures, informal self-initiated interpretation must prevail. Travelers might receive a looseleaf notebook which could serve to organize materials gathered during the trip, such as the social record, pamphlets, publications, and maps assembled by the passengers. The notebook would serve to direct information gathering, and upon completion it would contain a record of trip activities and participants.

Many sites at the pier complex are conducive to initial or continuing exchange of information among passengers, including waiting rooms, lobbies, agent offices, outdoor areas with views of the various ships, and check-in boarding lines. Miniexhibits and posters highlighting anticipated sites and events are possible at such places.

Early Sailing Northbound

While traveling north to Alaska, scenery, wildlife, shipboard events and all factors associated with the trip experience are of importance. These elements provide an overwhelming variety of stimuli, which passengers sample to become familiar with the new environment. Enthusiasm is high, the quest for information constant. However, as the passengers travel *through* the areas of interest, they actually experience little of the outside environment. Clark and Lucas (1978) compare this encapsulated travel to an "isolation booth" experience.

Passengers' intense interest in fishing boats, shipping traffic, and residents' relationship with the environment is an attempt to experience the authentic Alaskan environment. A trip log that includes a sequential map of the travel plan keyed to a periodically updated central map would serve this goal. The trip log could serve to pinpoint the position of the ship, which is of constant interest to passengers, and to identify settlements and waterways. The trip log also could include historical and cultural information, details of settlement patterns, and factual information regarding the major industries—forestry, fishing, and mining. Incorporating wildlife checklists, marine mammal surveys, and eagle counts would allow the "collection" aspects of the trip to be fulfilled.

An orientation movie and/or program on Alaska that provides an overview of the trip experience, anticipated stops, and wildlife should occur early in the cruise when passenger interest is highest. The amount of material presented at this time can be substantial; its range should be broad and include a great variety of topics.

Visiting Ports

During the several days of visitation to various ports of call and Glacier Bay, passengers' attention swings back and forth from information on ports to the social events onboard ship. After several days of traveling, the settlements passed, shipping and fishing fleet activity, and scenery cease to be novel, and little interest in them is noted for the majority of passengers.

In conjunction with land managers, the cruise ship company could develop a series of posters drawing attention to features on the trip; these could be rotated as the trip progresses. The ship's newspaper could be planned to highlight key elements of the trip. Bulletin boards prominently displayed could allow for information exchange among passengers and discussion of trip details. "Cruise cards" describing Alaskan scenery, wildlife, and history could be placed at the center of each table at evening meals, along with other information. The cards could be collected by travelers, especially if prepunched for insertion in their trip record notebook.

Because vicarious experiences with the resource are important for some, a key location for consolidating and verifying information is necessary. The ship's library could be stocked with relevant reading material on Alaska, including brochures and interpretive material on the Alaskan Interior that would be of interest to one-way passengers connecting with tours to these locations. Use of the trip log may prolong passenger interest in the ship's travel corridor by increasing the amount of information available. The pattern of decreasing interest observed currently occurs where no interpretive efforts are made; this pattern may change with provision of comprehensive interpretive programs.

More formal approaches at this phase include periodic updates given over the public address system regarding wildlife sightings and ship position. This and any other information, regardless of source, was promptly relayed to uninformed individuals, researchers observed. A similar phenomenon might be evident if prepared audio programs were broadcast over the ship's radio channels, so that passengers could listen in their cabins if they chose. Automated slide programs also could be set up in a central lounge.

Some passengers indicated they were unaware of activity alternatives in the ports of call. This gap could be filled by formal presentations or an informal question-and-answer meeting prior to each visitation. Such programs should be given by knowledgeable staff members or agency interpretive personnel. If a complete cruise with a single passenger group is not possible, interpreters could be present on one segment of the trip for each ship. After the manner of Alaska Marine Highway programming, each trip leg also could be theme-related. Travel up Lynn Canal to Skagway could focus on gold rush history and the Chilkoot Trail, while cruising to Sitka could highlight Russian-American history in the area. At present, onboard interpretation does not focus on the unique character and diversity of each location.

Successful employment of matching techniques in part depends on recognition and use of informal group processes that diffuse the interpretive message beyond those initially exposed to the material. A message is not received by an individual in isolation from social memberships: rather a person performs in a role appropriate to one's position in the participating group. In a leisure setting where an interpretive program is presented to groups, some persons may discuss topics for other group members, provide links between groups through information exchange, or transfer information to nonattenders during informal conversation. Attendance at structured programs may not accurately reflect the true impact of the information provided; secondary effects can be encouraged by development of unstructured interpretive aids peripheral to the core program.

Traveling Toward Home Port

Travel to Alaska includes both an informational and social component. Information gathering behavior is evident in the earlier stages of the cruise; certain attractions and species sightings are viewed as compulsory. Upon accomplishment of this "task," however, social goals predominate.

On the cruise home, the natural environment merely provides a backdrop for shipboard social events. Alaska is recounted in conversation and programs which serve as the recollection phase of the trip. Interpretation at this stage should thus focus on techniques which consolidate the information obtained and review the places visited. Booklets relating various Alaskan themes can fulfill the "take-home" phase of cruising. This provides an opportunity to collate the information received and makes it more easily recalled with the passage of time. In a study of tourism in Amish communities in Pennsylvania, Buck (1978) noted that reading publications subsequent to visitation reinforced the event and allowed for vicarious enjoyment.

Various interpretive themes have been proposed throughout this article. In summary, the following topics are suggested: industries, lifestyle, navigation aids, history, transportation networks, weather, tides, marine shorelife, whale migration, salmon spawning, native culture, U.S. Forest Service and National Park Service management, geology, flora, pipeline construction, and glacial geology.

Additionally, passengers returning from travels to the Interior and Far North could be encouraged to share their experience with passengers who did not visit these sites. The post-trip recollection phase at home would be furthered by later viewing of the trip record collections, and could be shared both among participants and with relatives and friends. The ability to easily recall highlights of the trip experience by accumulated material may increase the retention period and prolong overall satisfaction. Table 2 consolidates our description of the cruise environment and summarizes the level, message content, and method for interpretive alternatives.

Summary

Different interpretive options arise throughout the cruise ship experience, and this chapter has examined opportunities for matching different social phases and activities with appropriate interpretational material. Existing information networks involving the travel industry, resource agencies, and cruise participants all can be used as instruments for knowledge gathering and exchange. On a cruise ship the passengers are together for a relatively long period of time, and social networks and information channels become comparatively stabilized. This process is not unique to cruise ship travelers, however. There are other clientele populations which would exhibit similar behavior patterns. Organized group tours and extended hikes are two examples where potential development of social structure might occur. The self-contained nature of the cruise ship allows for progressive disclosure of interpretive material that builds upon previous presentations, and programs

Table 2. Description of cruise ship environment and interpretive options at each place

Phases of trip	Relationship to Alaska environment	Social networks formed	Level of interest	Message content	Alternative methods
Anticipation, planning, and travel to departure port	create images of Alaska, preparation for trip	cruise ship companies and traveling companies	builds toward departure; overview	clothes, weather, bibliography, addresses	pamphlets, guides, books
Embarkation	shipboard environment	initial group introductions	high; introductory	shipboard facilities and events	social record, mini-exhibits, posters
Early trip	all trip elements are stimuli	group formation	high; introductory	scenery, location, and wildlife	trip log, maps, orientation movie/program, trip record folder
Ports/Glacier Bay	alternating port/shipboard focus	communication established among new friends	moderate; focused	community/ Glacier Bay	ship newspaper, cruise cards, library, public address system, audio programs, movies, agency interpreters
Traveling toward home port	social events	friendships stabilized	low, synthesis	recollection and consolidation	booklets and pamphlets, other passengers

geared to this philosophy may also be appropriate for long-term repeat visitors to a recreation site.

Trip phasing occurs for all leisure activities. By coordinating interpretive efforts for a site or activity, material could be designed for use during a specific phase in the recreation process (e.g., pamphlets distributed to aid vacation planning), or for use during several phases. Current interpretive efforts focused primarily on the on-site experience need to be reexamined in light of the stages involved in a recreation experience. Preparatory information will assist potential visitors in selecting a site consistent with their desired experience, while material provided after site visitation may promote a continuing dialogue between recreationists and managers and provide feedback and evaluation.

The amount of information available changes behavior at recreational settings. On a cruise ship, passengers utilize fellow travelers as information sources in the absence of interpretation. By continued analysis of observed activity patterns, interpretive offerings can be matched to current behaviors, and periodic updates and modifications can make this program sensitive to both short-term and long-range management goals.

Section III

Essays

The sociological perspective also can be applied to a variety of contemporary issues that affect interpretation. The articles in this section are not studies *per se,* but essays on a wide range of topics. In the tradition of Tilden's principles, their purpose is to provoke the reader to view interpretation in a social context, to adopt the sociological "way of seeing" discussed at the beginning of the book.

In the first essay, "Social and Demographic Change: Implications For Interpretation," the focus is on how demographic trends and lifestyle changes may affect the interpreter's audience and what bearing these changes may have on the interpretive approach. The implication is that interpreters must monitor such changes and adjust their programs accordingly.

The second essay deals with a sociological process not widely discussed in earlier chapters—the interplay of myth, values, and behavior. Joseph Meeker's 1973 essay "Red, White and Black in the National Parks," first published in *The North American Review,* initiated a vigorous debate over the level of elitism found in U.S. National Parks. Perhaps overlooked was Meeker's insight that the very resources interpreters interpret are often cultural symbols of great potency. In a heterogeneous nation like the United States, it should not surprise us that some American subcultures are ambivalent toward historic sites, national parks, and other traditional settings for interpretation. The challenge that this creates for interpreters is significant.

"Interpretation in an Urban Society" is the third essay. Over 67 percent of the United States population lives in cities, and the implications for urban interpretation that stem from this statistic include a need to understand the role of nature in the city. The essay examines historical trends, the sociological functions of urban open space, and property rights and argues that all are factors influencing interpretive programming in urban areas.

The last essay is what the author, Kenneth Nyberg, has described as "friendly banter." First given at the Association of Interpretive Naturalists workshop in 1977, "Some Radical Comments on Interpretation" was viewed by some as controversial. Nyberg examines interpretation as an institutional function and challenges "the fundamental character of interpretation." The essay is included here because its analysis of interpretation is sociological (much of the essay dwells on the social relations between the interpreter and visitor), and because it speaks from the viewpoint of what the sociologist Peter Berger has called "the disenchanted observer." If interpretation is to advance as that unique public service Tilden envisioned, such disenchantment is healthy reading.

Social and Demographic Change: Implications for Interpretation

Darryll R. Johnson
Donald R. Field

Introduction

MANAGERS OF PUBLIC lands set aside for recreation are entering a period of unique challenge. They are confronted with fewer fiscal and personnel resources with which to protect natural and cultural resources and to maintain facilities and services. They are also participants in a technological revolution influencing park operations through the use of satellite communication systems and microcomputers to record and monitor budgets, personnel records, maintenance operations, resource inventories, and visitor use statistics. At the same time, managers are aware that the kind and number of people who visit parks and make recreational use of forests are changing. Foreign visitation is on the rise, demographic characteristics of the American population are different than only ten years ago, and some observers feel a different value orientation is emerging among a sizable proportion of Americans.

For the interpreter whose primary responsibility is to communicate natural and cultural history, these changes can be profound. Who are the new consumers of interpretive programs? What kind of recreational experiences do they seek? How important is the

Adapted from "Social Change and its Implications to Interpretation," by Darryll R. Johnson and Donald R. Field. (Paper presented at the Pacific Northwest Association of Interpretive Naturalists, Seattle, Washington, October 14-16, 1981). Portions are adapted from Darryll Johnson, "The U.S. Work Place in a Time of Social and Demographic Change," National Park Service Cooperative Park Studies Unit Paper Number One. Seattle: University of Washington, 1983.

transfer of information on natural and cultural history to their
recreational experience?

The purpose of this chapter is to highlight some of the social
and demographic trends altering the composition of the American
population who will visit parks and forests in the future. We begin
with a discussion of demographic trends in the American population.
Next we examine lifestyle and cultural value changes in American
society. Finally, we discuss the implications these changes have
for interpretation.

Demographic Factors

The American population is undergoing demographic changes
that are having and will continue to have an impact on many social
institutions, including those that provide recreational opportunities.
Changes in the age structure, changes in household composition,
the increased number of females in the labor force, and the urban-
to-rural migration are examples of factors that will alter the nature
and flow of people who utilize recreational services. Recreation
professionals who understand these changes will be in a better
position to respond in a proactive manner and thereby improve
their ability to serve clients, as well as to protect natural and
cultural resources.

A Nation Growing Old

The number and proportion of older people in American
society has been increasing throughout this century. In the early
part of the century, the United States was a "young" society. In
1900 only 4 percent of the population was over sixty-five. By
1980 this proportion had risen to 11.2 percent. Although the
current and future age structure of the United States has been
affected by increased survivorship of those born in the first quarter of this century, the most significant factor in altering the age
profile has been the decline in fertility from the Depression era to
the present. Soldo notes:

> A fall in fertility like that of the last 15 to 20 years in the U.S. reduces
> the proportion of young persons and thus increases the proportion
> of adults and older persons in the population. Declining mortality on

the other hand usually increases the relative number of children and adolescents, although this is no longer true in the U.S. (1980:8).

The proportion of older people in America is increasing, and barring mitigating factors (such as dramatic increase in the birth rate), this trend will continue. Assuming replacement-level fertility, the percentage of the population over sixty-five will peak in 2030 at 18 percent. Assuming below-replacement-level fertility, this proportion will reach 22 percent by 2030. The median age in the United States (twenty-five in 1920) is presently thirty and will peak at about thirty-eight in 2030.

The Baby Boom Population Becomes Adults. A primary result of the changing age structure will be the increasing number of middle-aged Americans as the baby boom generation enters its thirties in the next decade. The number of families headed by a person aged thirty-five to forty-four is projected to increase by 44 percent between 1980 and 1990. The number of families whose head is twenty-five to thirty-four years old is projected to increase by only 10 percent, and the number of families headed by a person under twenty-five is expected to decrease by 17 percent (Planning Economics Group 1981). These data suggest that proportionally more families will have higher incomes because of earning increases in the middle-aged years and the high number of families having both spouses working in this group. For example, one source projects the number of four-person households with incomes over $30,000 (in constant 1980 dollars) to increase 77 percent by 1990 (Data Resources, Inc. 1981). Families with incomes over $50,000 headed by persons aged thirty-five to forty-four will be one of the fastest growing groups. Those with incomes between $50,000 and $75,000 will increase 142 percent (from 1.4 to 3.4 million) and those with over $75,000 income will increase 214 percent (from 396 thousand to 1.24 million) (Data Resources, Inc. 1982).

Changes in Households and Families

The household in America is undergoing substantial structural change. One of the most important changes is simply the shrinking size of the average household.

114   *D. R. Johnson and D. R. Field*

Change in Average Household Size, 1790-1980   Persons

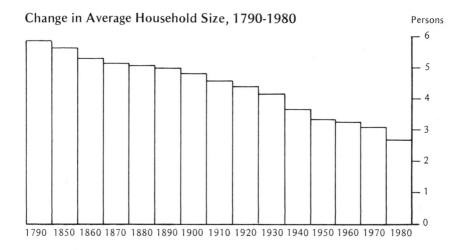

1790 1850 1860 1870 1880 1890 1900 1910 1920 1930 1940 1950 1960 1970 1980

Figure 1.   Change in average household size, 1790-1980. Reprinted with changes by permission from *American Demographics,* October 1981.

The Shrinking Household. Average household size decreased to 2.75 persons in 1980, falling from 3.11 in 1970 (Figure 1). During the same period, while the population grew 11.4 percent, the number of American families increased 27 percent. This increase was caused primarily by the number of persons living alone. Single people living alone increased 93 percent in this decade, and the number of divorced people living alone doubled (Russel 1981:28).

Fewer Children. According to the U.S. Census Bureau, married women at present expect to have an average of 2.2 children, down from 2.6 in 1971. The figure is highest for those without a high school diploma (2.4) and lowest for those with some graduate education (1.8). Further, significant numbers of women are opting to have no children at all. According to Pebley and Bloom, "The proportion of women who have never had a child has doubled, from 12 percent of never-married women 25 to 29 years old in 1965 to 25 percent in 1979." By some estimates, the number of women who never have a child will increase markedly. What is unknown is the number of young couples who intend not to have children but will later have them. This sector has recently resulted in an increase in the number of first births for women over thirty.

Divorce and the Single Parent Family. Divorce has increased at a high rate in the United States in recent years. The number of divorced people increased by 6 million between 1960 and 1979, going from 2.3 to 5.2 percent of the population. Population change accounts for about 1 million of the 6 million increase—meaning that 83 percent of the increase is due to social rather than demographic factors (Melko and Cargan 1981:30). Until twenty years ago the general divorce rate was reasonably constant—about eight or nine divorces per 1,000 married women aged fifteen and older. By 1967 the rate had risen slightly to about 11.2. But by 1979 the rate had doubled to 22.8 per thousand married women. Assuming constant divorce rates over the life of marriages performed at present, 50 percent will end in divorce (Weed 1982:17).

Most people who divorce remarry. A 1976 study of women aged fifteen to forty-four indicates that 70 percent of divorcees remarry within five years of their divorce. Forty-four percent of all marriages in 1979 were remarriages, compared to 30 percent in 1969 (Weed 1982:13).

There seems little reason to expect that divorce rates will decline in the near future. Arguing for decline is the fact that more people are waiting until later to marry, and later marriages last longer. On the other hand, the existing rates of divorce and remarriage suggest even higher divorce rates, because remarriages have a higher rate of failure. In addition, factors such as a wider acceptance of divorce in general and economic hard times may continue to be conducive to a high divorce rate.

Single-parent families (90 percent of which are headed by women), increased 49 percent between 1960 and 1970 and 76 percent between 1970 and 1978. In comparison, the number of families with two parents decreased by 3 percent in the 1970-1978 period (Bane and Weiss 1980:11).

Two-Income and Dual-Career Families

One of the most dramatic trends affecting both the family and the work world is the increasing number of American women in the labor force. Between 1968 and 1978, the number of two-earner families grew 4.5 million (25 percent), while the number of families in which the husband worked and the wife did not decreased by 4.0 million. In 1978 only 33 percent of all families were supported by the husband only (Hayghe 1981:35).

The demographic characteristics of families with working wives are quite distinct. Hayghe found that, "In 1978, husbands and wives in two-earner families were an average of seven years younger than their counterparts in traditional earner families" (1981:36). Between 1968 and 1978, women twenty to thirty-four years old accounted for two-thirds of the increase in married women in the work force. Fifty-eight percent of the two-earner families have children under 18, and 42 percent have preschool children. Significantly, families with two incomes have considerably higher incomes (Figure 2). Thirty-three percent of families with two earners had incomes over approximately $28,000, in comparison to 24 percent of those with one earner (Hayghe 1981).

As significant as the fact that more women are working are their attitudes toward work. In 1967, 44 percent of first-year college women and 67 percent of first-year college men thought a woman's place was at home. In 1970 only 10 percent of entering college women and 40 percent of all women accepted this view (Freeman 1979:71). Between 1971 and 1979, the percentage of working women who indicated they would continue to work if no longer necessary increased from 60 to almost 75 percent. These figures approximated male response to the same question (Campbell 1981:231). These changes suggest that some women are becoming more career oriented and no longer see their employment as supplemental income to a primary wage earner.

Urban-to-Rural Migration

Although it would be unwise to overemphasize its significance, migration to smaller cities and rural areas warrants consideration (however, the movement involves a relatively small number of people, and cities—by virtue of their size—continue to dominate the American scene). Until about 1970, there was a sustained migration of people from rural to urban and metropolitan areas. During this time and through the 1960s, metropolitan areas had

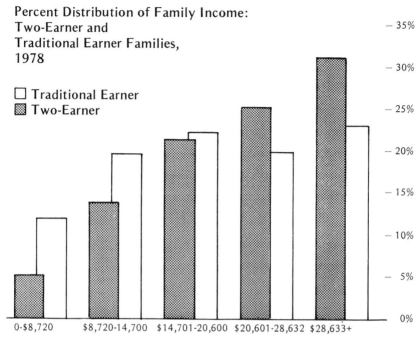

Percent Distribution of Family Income:
Two-Earner and
Traditional Earner Families,
1978

☐ Traditional Earner
▨ Two-Earner

Figure 2.　Distribution of family income for two-earner and traditional families, 1978. Reprinted with changes by permission from *American Demographics,* September 1981.

fairly high birth rates and were also the recipients of much internal migration. Jackson *et al.* note:

> During the 1960s, when birth rates in metropolitan areas were still high and people were still migrating in great numbers from farms and small towns to cities, metropolitan areas grew by 17 percent and non-metropolitan areas by 4.4 percent. During the 1970s, by contrast, metropolitan areas grew by 9.1 percent, while the population classified as non-metropolitan grew by 15.4 percent (1981:65).

Most of the metropolitan area growth during the 1970s occurred as a result of annexation and reclassification of nonmetropolitan counties. As this trend occurred, however, there was a growth of population in nonmetropolitan areas not entirely explained by expansion of metropolitan areas into nonmetropolitan counties.

The reasons for this movement are not entirely clear; survey data are limited. Clearly a partial cause is economic change. For example, opportunities for new jobs are occurring in areas where there were previously few. Economic variables, however, fail to account for all of this trend, strongly suggesting that quality of life considerations are at work.

In a midwestern study of metropolitan migrants to nonmetropolitan areas, Williams and Sofranko (1980) found that 65 percent of metropolitan migrants had moved to a genuinely rural area. Of those persons aged eighteen to fifty-nine in the study, more cited environmental or lifestyle factors than economic reasons (44 percent as compared to 35 percent) for their move. Most of the people interviewed in this study saw their move as pursuing a life goal rather than a job or economic opportunity. While the Williams and Sofranko study may not be representative of all metropolitan migration, the findings are consistent with changes in cultural values noted by other writers.

Lifestyles and Cultural Values

Overlying demographic change is evidence of fundamental value shifts among a significant portion of Americans. Because of changes in the American economy, Yankelovich (1981) asserts that increasing numbers of Americans are growing doubtful about their ability to share in the American dream of ever increasing affluence. According to Yankelovich (1981:39), in "the decade between the late sixties and the late seventies the number of Americans who believe hard work always pays off fell from a 58 percent majority to a 43 percent minority."

Similarly, the percentage of people agreeing with the statement "work is at the center of my life" declined from 34 percent to 13 percent. This shift, combined with the value changes that began among youth in the 1960s, are said to be leading to dramatic cultural changes in what Yankelovich (1981:8) calls "the unwritten rules governing what we give in marriage, work, community, and sacrifice for others and what we expect in return." Yankelovich also notes:

Throughout most of this century, Americans believed that self-denial made sense, sacrifice made sense, obeying the rules made sense, subordinating the self to the institution made sense. But doubts have set in, and Americans now believe that the old giving/getting compact needlessly restricts the individual while advancing the power of large institutions—government and business, particularly—who use the power to enhance their own interests . . .

This judgement . . . has now been made by the overwhelming majority of the American people—ranging from 70 to 80 percent. Each person's life experiment is designed to change the giving/getting compact of private life, but the sum of tens of millions of life experiments transform public life as well. These experiments have the makings of a true cultural revolution because the new shared meaning they introduce—the assumption that it is wrong to subordinate the sacred/expressive side—has an awesome power to change our lives.

The new shared meaning bears a resemblance to the old one. The old one said, poverty is not destiny. The new one says, instrumentalism is not destiny. The old meaning insisted that political freedom can coexist with material wellbeing and indeed enhance it. The new meaning insists that the personal freedom to shape one's life can coexist with the instrumentalism of modern technological society and can civilize it (1981:231).

It is important to understand that this potential value revolution is not an exercise in unrestrained self-indulgence. In fact, Yankelovich sees increasing numbers of people viewing the excesses of the 1960s as "candidates for the junk-heap" and self-defeating. This rejection of 1960s hedonism, however, does not mean a return to a previous ethic of self-denial, nor does it mean a rejection of material affluence. The emerging morality is functioning to bring individual wants and societal needs to a compatible blend. It "is now gathering force around two kinds of commitments: closer and deeper friendships, and the switch from certain instrumental values for expressive ones"* (Yankelovich, 1981:250).

---

* One is being instrumental when one asks about something, "What is it good for?" For example, a tree may be valued for its timber rather than as good in itself (sacred). Likewise people can be seen as objects or valuable in themselves—simply as individual people.

Seventy percent of Americans indicate they have many acquaintances and few friends; 41 percent say they have fewer friends than in the past. In 1973, 32 percent of Americans "felt an intense need to compensate for the impersonal and threatening aspects of modern life by seeking mutual identification with others based on close ethnic ties or ties of shared interests, needs, backgrounds, ages or values." By the beginning of the 1980s this figure had increased to 47 percent (Yankelovich 1981:251). The search for more meaningful social ties and the rejection of both the "me first" and self-denial ethics are said to be resulting in a new ethic of commitment:

> . . . the new ethic of commitment pursues the goal of striking a better balance between the instrumental and the sacred/expressive aspects of life. It does so through a willingness to sacrifice those material/ instrumental values that inhibit the sacred/expressive ones. The sacrifice generally involves money or status . . .
>
> People also speak of abandoning instrumental values in favor of a closer relationship to land, plants, mountains, oceans, and nature in general . . .
>
> All over the country, Americans are weighing the rewards of conventional success against less lucrative but more satisfying personal achievements, and are choosing, or seriously considering the latter—if they can afford to do so (Yankelovich 1981:234).

How many individuals consider self-fulfillment a paramount life goal, and who are they? In a national sample of working Americans, Yankelovich (1981) identified a group of "strong formers" who are most completely involved in the quest for self-fulfillment and who represent one end of a continuum characterizing self-conscious construction of life around the moral virtue of self-expression. This group is about 17 percent of the population. They tend to be younger, more highly educated, professional, less apt to be married, liberal in their politics, and more likely to have no religious affiliations. When asked to choose between living "more creative lives" or being better off financially, the strong formers chose the more creative life by a two to one margin. These figures were reversed for the rest of the population.

The term "creativity" took on many meanings among the strong former group. Among these were stronger emphasis on leisure, more interest in spending money on experiences rather than tangible possessions, efforts to acquire self-understanding, and the general emphasis upon individuality. Significantly, strong formers wanted to be successful in their careers to a larger extent than others but were also committed to working hard at self-fulfillment (66 percent).

Of those outside the strong former group, Yankelovich believes approximately 63 percent make up a "weak former" group, and 20 percent adhere to traditional values and norms. The weak formers, while embracing older success goals, may have internalized aspects of newer ideas of self-fulfillment that lead them to question life's purpose and meaning, including aspects of their work. However, a substantial minority (20 percent) of Americans find their lives relatively unaffected by the cultural shifts of the recent past, and their lifestyles mirror those of the 1950s and earlier.

Social and Demographic Change: Implications for the Interpreter

The demographic and cultural elements of social change discussed here should be of interest to recreation professionals—particularly to interpreters. The changing age structure suggests a trend toward more older and affluent middle-aged people and a middle-aged population greatly influenced by the events of the 1960s. The former baby-boomers are much more sophisticated than older cohorts regarding the media to which they have been exposed. Interpreters may need to reexamine their various delivery systems to capture the attention of these new clients. The use of microcomputers in interpretation should be explored. For example, information on the flora and fauna of a park could be stored in a computer file where it would be accessible to visitors desiring detailed information on a given species. Digitized maps derived from satellite imagery could be used in visitor centers to illustrate ecological change.

Parks and forests have traditionally attracted the more vigorous and healthy retirees. Thus, land managers can expect to see an increase in this segment of their visitor populations. Shorter walks and more frequent walks may be desired. An expansion of early morning and daytime programs could be considered. Outdoor recreational activities oriented toward the young will have a smaller market segment than during the last fifteen years.

Touring and organized tours will likely increase. Interpreters may want to expand both audio and visual packaged programs for use on a variety of public transport systems offered in conjunction with these visits. Orientation programs to the cultural and/or natural history of the area could be provided during travel to an area, while prepackaged programs are provided to groups on-site. Upon exit, a summary program could connect individual places or events experienced during the stay.

Changes in the family structure are particularly important. Interpreters may increasingly find that material aimed at the conventional family is only marginally relevant to a large clientele. Many young families may have no children, and many may have only one parent. Other groups, such as older widowed women, may become more common in parks and other outdoor recreational areas.

Changes in cultural values combined with demographic factors (such as the changing age structure, changing family structure, and two-career families) mean an increasing diversity in the type of people interpreters must serve. For example, in national parks, many visitors will fit the traditional mold—urban middle-aged families with young children. But many will not. The interpreter will increasingly need skills in interpersonal communication, as the situation demands more discrimination in terms of the audience at hand. The development of a diversity of programs for a diversity of groups may become the dominant interpretive planning guideline.

In some outlying areas, the urban-to-rural migration may change the nature of the local constituency frequenting outdoor recreation areas. For example, on the Olympic Peninsula in Washington, new residents (who are mostly ex-urbanites attracted to the rural atmosphere and physical attractiveness of the area) have different values and expectations regarding recreational opportunities on publicly managed lands than longtime residents (many of whom were dependent upon the forest products industry). Knowledge of changing local population will enhance the opportunities to convey new park policies, prepare public involvement programs, introduce new interpretive programs, and facilitate relationships between parks and their neighbors. The ties between recreation agencies and local communities are increasingly important, and the role of the interpreter will be crucial in developing this partnership.

Changes in the Interpretive Workforce

Organizations that provide interpretive services will be increasingly affected by changing social forces. The evolving value system is bringing changes in many areas, but three are particularly important: (1) the increasing importance of leisure and the growing interest in spending money on experiences rather than tangible possessions, (2) the symbolic importance of a paid job for women, and (3) the insistence that jobs become less depersonalized and more meaningful (i.e., more self-fulfilling). According to Yankelovich (1978), only one in five persons surveyed states that work is more important than leisure. Sixty percent say that they enjoy their work but it is not their major source of satisfaction. All of these factors will affect the men and women who become interpreters in the future.

As the role of housewife declines in status, the world of work becomes more important to women as a source of self-esteem, independence, and autonomy. As a result, women will probably be more discriminating about the nature of jobs they are willing to take as they accept the values of the traditional male-dominated work world (Yankelovich 1979:14).

The rejection of the work role as the core of identity for increasing numbers of people will also change the nature of future employees. Americans increasingly expect to be recognized as unique individuals rather than objects in bureaucratic slots. Being recognized as an individual and working with likable people may be an important expectation in the workplace. The drive to work hard at any job under any circumstances may decrease, requiring the employer to provide new incentives. The need for different incentives may be especially noticeable for men if the cultural meaning of masculinity changes, and as women enter the workforce in increasingly better paying jobs that diversify sources of family income.

Employees will increasingly bring with them diverse personal situations. Out of the material presented in this discussion, the following are examples of factors that may be of concern.

1. Increasing numbers of midcareer workers and more competition for promotion and salary increases.
2. Potential shortages of young workers.
3. Increasing numbers of older workers (with the legal right to employment until age 70).
4. Increasing numbers of complex employee family situations involving divorced parents, single-parent families, and two-career families.
5. Increasing numbers of women in the workplace with higher career expectations.
6. Emerging shifts in cultural values, such as decreasing emphasis on work as a source of money, status, and power and increasing emphasis on work as a component of self-fulfillment.
7. Possible increasing resistance to relocation due to dual-career families, economic difficulties, and unwillingness to sever personal and community ties.

Following the intuitively simple notion that good personnel management links organizational objectives to personal needs of employees, it follows that interpersonal communication skills will be increasingly important as individuals search for satisfying working situations that also fulfill organizational objectives. In matching the needs of individuals and the organization, diverse work arrangements will be more common: flexible work time, compressed work time, job sharing, wider sharing of responsibility for job content, retraining of older workers, partial retirement schemes, and more opportunity for sabbaticals and education, to name a few. Coordinating such arrangements requires a personal level of communication that is ongoing and open, with the immediate supervisor being an important link to the organization.

We are led to the conclusion that efficiency in the workplace may rest more and more on the success of human communication that links the individual and the organization in a meaningful way. If this conclusion is correct, out of the current cultural change and ambiguity may come a solution to one of mankind's most persistent dilemmas—the search for a process to realize the common good while protecting and enhancing the freedom and dignity of the individual. In organizations where they are present, interpreters could play an important role in enhancing and improving this internal communication.

Conclusion

Social change today is rapid and far-reaching. The role of the interpreter as a communication specialist may be important in a broader range of responsibilities than previously imagined. For too long, interpreters have been trained in a narrow band of disciplines usually related to specific natural, cultural and/or historic resources. The need for greater sensitivity and understanding of interpersonal relationships, the value orientation of consumers, human behavior patterns, new social environments, and the way culture affects visitors' adaptation to parks has hampered successful communication between professionals and clients. The more that interpreters know about the people they serve, the more effective interpretation will be.

Red, White, and Black in National Parks

Joseph W. Meeker

NATIONAL PARKS WERE created as an expression of deeply rooted but poorly understood values inherent in American culture and in the traditions of Western civilization. No one need be surprised if ethnic groups who do not share those values fail to see the parks as their founders did, or as the National Park Service might like them to. It is worthwhile to review some of the myths and images relevant to park lands in Western culture in order to measure their distance from the traditions of minority groups in America.

Nature as a Refuge

The Western world has long looked on nature as a symbol of peace and purity. The garden of Eden was a natural setting characterized by beauty, simplicity, and moral innocence until it was infiltrated by corrupting influences. Ancient Greek thought also idealized a "Golden Age" somewhere in the dim past, conceived as a garden where food was abundant and adversity unknown. Both the Greek and Hebraic roots of Western culture agree that man originated in a benevolent garden and that civilization is a debased condition intended to punish man. When he was expelled from the benevolent garden, man went forth to build the ugly and hostile cities where he now suffers.

Efforts to regain the lost garden as a refuge from urban life have long occupied our minds. We dream of safe natural settings which will provide the comfort and repose lacking in the city. Such nostalgia for nature is common in our time, but it is also

Reprinted with permission from *The North American Review,* © 1973 by the University of Northern Iowa.

found strongly among the urban aristocrats of ancient Rome. The Roman poet Virgil is remembered not only for the *Aeneid,* but also for his pastoral poetry which glorifies the peace and simplicity of the rural countryside in contrast to the anxieties of urban life in Rome. And Juvenal, a Roman satirist of the second century A.D., speaks of "Rome, the great sewer" because of its pollution problems, then proceeds with a long list of other Roman miseries, including degrading poverty in the ghettos, high taxes, inflated prices for poor goods and services, corrupt government, crime and vice in the streets, pressures of social conformity in the suburbs, and poor schools run by wicked teachers. Juvenal's advice to weary Romans is "Tear yourself from the games and get a place in the country" where life will be easier, safer, and more sensible. Our culture has long agreed with Juvenal and Virgil that city life degrades man and that the country restores his sense of dignity; in the city man is controlled, but in the country he controls. Rural settings have symbolized both the purity of nature and the power of man since the beginning of the Western cultural tradition.

It may seem a paradox that the love of nature has been strongest in those civilizations which have produced the largest cities and the most complex technologies. From ancient Rome to modern America, nature has been thought of as a refuge from the problems of civilization. Within that tradition, humans have expected to find in natural settings a reaffirmation of human worth and purity. Like Adam and Eve in their garden, park visitors often feel their personal sanctity when they enter natural surroundings, and they feel the loss of sanctity when they return to the profane life awaiting them in the city. Nature is not sacred, but humans feel sanctified by their contact with nature. Such attitudes are not found among the hunting and agricultural cultures of Africa and the American Indians, where *nature itself* is thought sacred, and humans participate in that sacredness according to their degree of integration with natural processes. The need to protect nature from human activities is thus strongest in those cultures where humans look upon themselves as separate from natural life, and where they see that civilization is dangerous to the natural settings they need for spiritual relief.

The Royal Privilege

The recreational enjoyment of natural surroundings has been until recently a privilege reserved for aristocratic classes. Since Roman times, only those with wealth and leisure have been free to escape the pressures of the city. The great park lands of Europe were originally established as royal game preserves and forests from which commoners were strictly barred. British common law held that wildlife and forests belonged to the crown, as Robin Hood discovered when he poached the king's deer. The American translation of this tradition specifies that wild lands and animals belong to the people as a whole, but the idea of state ownership was long established by European monarchs before America appeared on the scene.

Early settlers in North America looked upon the land as a natural refuge from the oppressive cities of Europe. America was thought of from the beginning as a gigantic garden or wilderness park where humans could regulate their lives according to the principles of nature rather than the whims of kings. America *was* a national park in the minds of our founding fathers, but one which existed for the benefit of all people rather than merely a handful of royalty.

Yet, strangely, the aristocratic view of gardens remained alive as our early history unfolded. The leaders of the American Revolution were members of a new kind of aristocracy that was also based on land ownership. They shared the view that a social utopia would be created if the values traditionally associated with gardens and farms could somehow be fused with the needs of civilized life. Thomas Jefferson envisioned a civilization which would draw its moral strength from the people's attachment to the land. In Jefferson's words, "Those who labor in the earth are the chosen people of God . . . whose breasts he has made his peculiar deposit for substantial and genuine virtue." Jefferson, of course, was not thinking of the American Indians or of the black slaves who labored in the earth of the plantations, but rather of farmer-landowners like himself—the pastoral gentlemen who owned and managed the American garden. Jefferson connected both moral virtue and political rights to land stewardship exercised by landowners. Slaves and Indians, no matter how close they might be to the land, were excluded from Jefferson's vision and from the Constitution which he and his fellow proprietors created.

Snakes and Machines in the Garden

Jefferson feared the intrusion of a snake into the American garden, and he knew that the snake's name was industry. Leo Marx's revealing book, *The Machine in the Garden* (1964), traces Jefferson's anguish as he fought the development of manufacturing and industry in the hope of preserving the garden qualities of America. Jefferson even argued that America should export raw materials to Europe for manufacture and import finished products rather than develop factories on the garden soil of America. He knew that the machine and the garden were incompatible.

Jefferson's hopes for retaining a garden America dissolved, Leo Marx tells us, when the War of 1812 made it necessary to develop manufacturing in the interests of national defense. Like Adam in the Garden of Eden, America then fell from its state of purity, and Jefferson wrote in his diary that "Our enemy has indeed the consolation of Satan on removing our first parents from Paradise: from a peaceable and agricultural nation, he makes us a military and manufacturing one." Expelled from the garden by the two-headed snake of war and industry, we proceeded to build more and more machines in the garden, but Americans have never lost their sense of nostalgia and regret for the pastoral peace left behind.

The middle years of the nineteenth century were devoted to the machine and to the conversion of the wilderness garden into an efficient farm. Power and wealth appeared along with cities and industry, and America became more urban each year as it overwhelmed the natural wilderness with mechanical progress. Those who still cherished the dream of a garden America then organized themselves to preserve some part of that vision from the encroachment of machine America, and the national park idea was born in 1872 at Yellowstone.

America's national parks are expressive of myth that has been present in Western culture for some 4,000 years. They are National Gardens of Eden where we can feel close to the origins of human life and to the peace, innocence, and moral purity that myth ascribes to the origins of mankind. They are also places to seek refuge from cities and machines, offering us the psychological relief (the literal meaning of re-creation) that makes it possible to continue our work in unpleasant urban surroundings. They are remnants of the Jeffersonian dream of a garden Utopia, comforting for the evidence they offer that there are still a few places where the machine has not yet spoiled nature. And somewhere within us, they also feed our aristocratic ego by showing the world that we are rich and powerful enough to afford gardens. All Americans can think of themselves as kings who control vast game preserves.

The Roots of Minority Indifference

It is a source of some embarrassment and concern to National Park Service officials that the parks have never appealed equally to all people. Poor people, black people, and ethnic minorities generally show little enthusiasm for the park idea. Despite recent strenuous efforts to bring "Parks to the People," the parks remain essentially playgrounds for middle-class citizens. The reasons behind minority indifference toward national parks are largely unexplored, perhaps because indifference doesn't demand to be understood as strongly as hostility does. No minority groups really hate the parks, but none seem to care much about them either. Recent attempts at cultural self-appraisal by thoughtful black and Indian writers offer some insight into American minorities' lack of enthusiasm for parks.

First, it is important to remember that the Myth of the Gardens is not part of either African or American Indian traditions. The mythologies of both cultures assume that the civilized structures of human life are perfectly compatible with systems of nature, and both emphasize that the adaptation of human affairs to natural processes is one of the essential responsiblities of civilization. Before Africa and Indian America were influenced by the intrusions of European civilization, neither had ever heard that nature is a place of refuge from the evils of civilization, or that the present state of humanity represents a fall from an earlier state of purity symbolized by the garden. It is thus no wonder that the great national parks created by white men in Africa and America have always been difficult for the natives of both places to understand. Their inherited mythology simply does not support the idea of separate value systems for nature and for humanity.

In addition to their varying cultural mythologies, the red man and the black man have more practical reasons to view the American wilderness differently than white Americans. For the past few centuries, both groups have learned in pain that their association with the land is a source of misery and humiliation, not peace or fulfillment. Black and Indian values today not only lack the pastoral garden imagery reflected in the national parks, but both are in some ways actively hostile to that imagery.

Black Prisoners on the Land

Shortly after his release from prison in 1968, Eldridge Cleaver wrote an essay called "The Land Question and Black Liberation" (1970), in which he pointed out that one of the more important consequences of slavery in America was that "black people learned to hate the land." The American land was a place of punishment and imprisonment for slaves, not the source of liberation that white settlers found. From a black point of view, Jefferson's idyllic image of the nobility of rural gardens was thus completely reversed. The history of black people in America has tied them to the land with hatred, not love, with servitude rather than ownership. That is why, according to Cleaver, "one of the most provocative insults that can be tossed at a black is to call him a farm boy, to infer that he is from a rural area or in any way attached to an agrarian situation" (1970:18). Since the end of official slavery gave blacks some mobility, they have "come to measure their own value according to the number of degrees they are away from the soil" (1970:18). The city and its symbols, Cleaver concludes, are more likely to attract black allegiance than any images of nature.

Black efforts over the past few decades have been concentrated on the struggle for social justice and political power, not for relief or a pastoral retreat from pain. When refuge is needed from that struggle, black people are not likely to look for it in any wilderness setting, but among other black people, where they can expect to find understanding and human compassion. Nature, parks, and wilderness are terms that rarely appear in black vocabularies. A search among scores of recent books by black authors reveals no reference or index entry concerning national parks or wilderness lands. For most black people, the word park refers to an urban setting containing basketball courts, baseball diamonds, and perhaps a lawn for picnicking. The only wilderness of any concern is of the kind found in cities, the wilderness of the ghetto.

The Humiliation of American Indians

Indians, too, need to be free of the images historically imposed upon them by the white man. Vine Deloria, one of the most articulate Indian spokesmen of recent years, summed up in a nutshell the traditional white view of both blacks and Indians: "Negroes were considered draft animals, Indians wild animals" (1969:171). White images pictured the slave as a domesticated animal laboring in the American garden, and the Indian was viewed as a wild brother to the deer, antelope, and other creatures who were at home on the range. When national parks were established to commemorate the white conquest of the American wilderness and its wild animals, Indians were of course included. So now we can see bears at Yellowstone, wolves at Mount McKinley, Hopis at Grand Canyon, and Navajos weaving blankets at many national monuments of the southwest.

The national parks are places of humiliation for Indians who are displayed and exploited there. The curio counters are piled high with cheap imitations of Indian artifacts to be sold as trinkets to white tourists, and in the evening the naturalist's lecture is likely to begin with a brief description of the quaint Indians and other animals who used the parklands before the white man arrived. Many of the parks specifically glorify the white conquest over Indians or commemorate the white appropriation of Indian lands. Even the few preserved Indian victories are monuments to white dominance, as at Custer Battlefield, where it is shown how the Indians won the battle while losing the war. As the plantations remind blacks of both past and present causes for shame, so the parks often recall to Indians the destruction of their cultural heritage.

Economic and Social Problems

It is small wonder, then, that neither blacks nor Indians show enthusiasm for national parks. The usual explanation for their disinterest, common among sociologists and National Park Service officials, is of course also pertinent: blacks and Indians are generally poor people who can ill afford the time or money needed for enjoyment of nature, and neither group is likely to find much pleasure in the hiking, camping, photography, and nature study which attract middle-class whites to the parks. But even if blacks and Indians could be "taught" to appreciate parklands in the same way that many whites do, and even if both groups could somehow be provided sufficient wealth and leisure to visit the parks regularly, only the protruding tip of an enormous iceberg of indifference would be melted. The larger influence of established cultural values which disagree with those of white Americans would remain untouched.

Can the great wilderness parks, then, be of any benefit to American blacks and Indians, as Park Service officials now say they would like them to be? Perhaps not, except in the relatively superficial matter of providing inexpensive recreational space without discrimination for those few blacks and Indians who may choose to use the parks on weekend outings. The deeper emotional and cultural needs of both groups are unlikely ever to be satisfied in the sense that the parks satisfy Americans of European ancestry. Neither blacks nor Indians are ever likely to find the Garden of Eden in Yosemite Valley as other tourists do. Attempts by the National Park Service to attract minorities to the parks assume that these groups will find them pleasant and meaningful in the same way that white middle-class visitors do, but that assumption is most likely false.

Social Protest in the Wilderness

The national parks fortunately have not so far been involved in the great struggles between races and economic classes that have characterized recent decades. It is possible to imagine, however, a sad day when the wilderness parks might become just one more symbol of white American exploitation, as white banks and businesses now are to many young people of racial minorities. The parks do represent white American values, not universal human values, and there is no reason for them to be held sacred by groups who may oppose those values. A bit of plastic explosive in Old Faithful would go a long way as a protest demonstration. The features preserved in the parks are delicate and difficult to defend against those who do not respect them. If it should ever become fashionable to bomb and burn the national parks, we will have reached a profound and perhaps irreversible level of cultural and racial warfare. The very values which Americans have attached to the parks have made them vulnerable symbols of white exclusiveness, and so subject to such attacks.

The national parks need not be thought of as Gardens of Eden tended primarily for aristocratic or middle-class relaxation, or as symbols of the white man's conquest over nature or his fellow man, or as playgrounds for relief or distraction from urban social ills. Their most important values may lie instead in the integrity of the wilderness ecosystems which are protected within them, quite apart from any emotional needs they may satisfy for the American people. Wilderness ecosystems are capable of maintaining their equilibrium without human laws or intervention, and they represent our best source of information about the necessary preconditions for long-term survival of complex living communities. It is perhaps time now to look to our parks for the knowledge inherent in their natural structures, rather than for relief from the private fears we bring into them.

Ecology vs. Justice

Social justice and environmental stability are the two urgent needs facing American policy in the remaining decades of this century. Often their demands seem mutually exclusive, as when minority groups demand new industrial developments which will produce more jobs and more pollution, or when attempts at population control are regarded by racial minorities as genocide.

As the implications of both movements begin to unfold more fully in public, positions of neutrality between them will be more and more difficult to hold. The National Park Service, like most federal agencies, has so far elected to respond to the demands for social justice made by racial minorities, for that demand has been voiced most powerfully. The parks are increasingly expected to respond to legitimate social demands, even if a few demands of nature must be sacrificed in the process. The pendulum of Park Service policy, which has always swung precariously between preservation and recreation, seems now to be caught increasingly on the recreation side, and the imperative of preserving park wilderness must suffer accordingly. But that is a hopeless position for park policy to take. For even if the parks could be made accessible to all oppressed people in America, many of those people would not want the parks.

Racial prejudice is an internal disease of society that has grown from faulty human attitudes toward other humans. Environmental degradation is the sad result of mistaken human attitudes toward the processes of nature. Ecosystems, like racial minorities, have now announced to the white man that they will tolerate no more of his garbage or exploitation. Both crises have been created by the inordinate egotism of white culture with its demand for symbols of power and dominance; yet the two diseases should not be confused with one another, for their treatments must be different.

The goals of social justice will not be served by converting our best remaining examples of environmental integrity—the national parks—into settings for mass recreation. Prejudice and discrimination must be overcome by improving the laws and customs that govern human social relationships, not merely by providing minority groups with the recreational escapes which have sometimes helped white men to forget their problems. Similarly, environmental disease cannot be treated if we sacrifice our few surviving healthy ecosystems to social purposes. We will desperately need parks and other wilderness lands to study for the knowledge they alone contain about the ingredients essential to equilibrium among biological species, including our own species.

Black people and Indians have much to teach white culture about both problems. Both groups have survived tenaciously against overwhelming odds, because they have learned better than whites how to encourage tolerance and brotherhood among humans and how to adapt human activities to the conditions of natural environments. Both know that men must change in order to agree with the world, not the other way around. That is a lesson the white man has yet to learn from his fellow humans and from the wilderness land that still persists.

Interpretation in an Urban Society

Gary E. Machlis

IN 1979, MORE THAN 67 percent of the United States population resided in metropolitan areas, with 28 percent living in the central cities (U.S. Dept. of Commerce 1980). The city is home for a majority of Americans, and its consumption of food, energy, water, resources, and open space is significant. This suggests that nature in the city is both ecologically important and sociopolitically relevant. This essay is about nature in the city, how nature is interpreted, and how it can be interpreted for the urban population. An assumption is that interpretive programs in metropolitan areas require a knowledge of historical and contemporary urban trends.

The essay is organized into three sections. First, some of the unique characteristics of nature in the city are described. These vary by culture, but there seem to be regularities among metropolitan areas of Western industrial societies. The analysis then suggests implications of these trends for urban interpretation. Lastly, an attempt is made to define, in the broadest terms, the scope of nature interpretation in an urban society.

Nature in the City

Cities are complex systems comprised of people, social institutions, technologies, and natural environments (Hawley, 1971; Berry and Kasarda 1977; Michelson 1976). The city is both an outward form—housing, streets, factories, parks—and an inward pattern of life—cycles of work and play, routes of travel, rules of conduct, and so forth. Imbedded in both the physical form and social patterns of the city are its "nature areas"—those places

Adapted from "Interpretation in an Urban Society," by Gary E. Machlis. (Paper presented at the Pacific Northwest Association of Interpretive Naturalists, Seattle, Washington, October 14-16, 1981).

where flora and fauna are evident. If we focus on only the broadest trends, we can discern several unique characteristics of nature in the city.

1. *There is limited interdependence between local nature and other components of the urban system.* During the Neolithic stages of urbanization, the emerging cities of the Indus Valley and Fertile Crescent relied heavily on local ecosystems. These cities utilized organic sources of energy and local supplies of drinking water. Cultivated land was within walking distance of the urban center. Human and animal wastes were used as fertilizers. Low concentrations of inorganic refuse (such as glass and metal) were produced. The Neolothic city survived off the bounty provided by local ecosystems and was limited by their capacity.

A variety of technological and organizational advances released the urban settlement from reliance on local nature. The paved road made transport independent of season; the granary and reservoir allowed the storage of food and water. Concentration of administrative and military power (its physical form exemplified by the buttressed wall) allowed the city to conquer other populations and draw resources from more distant ecosystems. The limits of local nature were overthrown, yet enclaves of natural phenomena persisted. Even in the Middle Ages, cities retained some portion of land within their walls for use as gardens.

In the modern city, the actual interdependence between the urban population and its natural areas is relatively small. The majority of food, water, energy, and other resources comes from locations geographically distant; the city relies on what Catton (1980) calls "ghost acreage." New Yorkers draw water from upstate, eat vegetables from California, and drink orange juice from Florida. The large natural areas of most cities are either limited to providing recreation (e.g., parks) or acting as a convenient sink for industrial wastes (e.g., riverfronts). The smaller areas are often engulfed by economic processes that limit their usefulness. Martindale describes the impact of speculation and development on the growth of American cities:

> The inorganic gridiron plan of city lay-out was adapted to speculation and sale, for the first step in the development of a new quarter of the town was the plotting of streets . . . As the pattern extended, it

was accompanied by the destruction of the natural properties of open space. Low places and streams were filled in. The first step in preparing a site for real estate speculation was the clearing away of all or most of the natural features of the area (1960:172).

The ecological implications are significant: landfill, drainage, construction, and pollution act to reduce the viability and diversity of urban wildlife (Howard 1974) and can eliminate taxonomically important species (Campbell 1974). In some twentieth century urban areas (such as European ghettos of the late 1930s or high-rise developments of the 1950s), natural features simply disappeared.

2. *The city tends to collect and display nonlocal nature.* Metropolitan areas are centers of commerce, administration, education, and entertainment (Odum and Moore 1938; Zelinsky 1973). They concentrate and mix social elements from varied hinterlands. As an extension of this pattern, the city collects and displays nonlocal nature, and the urban population's interest often is in the exotic. Zoos and aquariums are examples. The ancient city of Rome was treated to an expanding menagerie of animals from conquered lands, and the Roman games consumed immense numbers of wildlife. At the dedication of the Colosseum under Titus, 9,000 animals were destroyed in 100 days (Hughes 1975). Feathers, bone, and hide were items of cosmopolitan fashion.

Nineteenth century cities also reveled in nonlocal nature. The great European and American circuses, major zoological collections, and arboretums were all elements of urban life. A variety of natural history lectures, poetry recitals, and travelogues were available as part of the lyceum movement, and these also helped satisfy the urbanite's fascination with nature from somewhere else (Dulles 1965).

Besides the traditional zoo and aquarium, other collections are unique to metropolitan regions. Amusement parks and public housing developments tend to landscape with nonlocal flora, and even the playfields of local parks may represent an exotic ecological community, held together by repeated fertilizing, reseeding, and artificial watering. Plant stores and pet shops reach many city dwellers, marketing nonlocal nature for private use.

3. *There are distinctive patterns that guide the use of urban natural areas, especially parks.* A variety of authors have at-

tempted to discern the unique characteristics of urban recreation (for a review, see Dunn 1980). These characteristics include distinct cycles of park use, norms for social interaction, and territorial boundaries that separate park users by age, class, or ethnic group (Lee 1972). The city park may be a source of social integration allowing friends to meet, couples to court, and gangs to assemble (Machlis et al. 1981).

Of these variables, it is social integration that is most distinctly cosmopolitan. The sociologist Durkheim (1947) saw the high densities of urban life as leading to a division of labor that allowed for high personal freedom; in return, mechanisms for integrating the

Table 1.   Social change in a metropolitan community (informal social participation)

Frequency of getting together with—	Percentage distribution	
	1959	1971
Relatives (other than those living at home with you):		
Every day, or almost every day	7	6
Once or twice a week	35	31
A few times a month	21	20
Once a month	12	14
A few times a year	14	20
Less often	4	5
Never	7	4
	100	100
Neighbors:		
Every day, or almost every day	13	12
Once or twice a week	19	17
A few times a month, or once a month	23	20
A few times a year, or less often	22	23
Never	23	28
	100	100
People you or your husband work with:		
Once or twice a week, or more often	15	14
A few times a month, or once a month	22	24
A few times a year, or less often	36	34
Never	27	28
	100	100
Friends who are not neighbors or fellow workers:		
Once or twice a week, or more often	25	19
A few times a month, or once a month	37	36
A few times a year, or less often	29	28
Never	9	7
	100	100

Source: Duncan, Schuman, and Duncan (1973:46).

urban population were required. Table 1 shows the stability of such behaviors. A study of the Detroit metropolitan area in 1959 and 1971 suggests remarkable regularities in the frequency of interactions between relatives, neighbors, and others. Little variation was apparent over a decade marked by urban riots, student rebellions, assassinations, and moon walks (Cheek and Burch 1976). Social integration, it seems, remains an urban imperative.

The city's natural areas have traditionally provided an arena for this social phenomenon. Lovers' lanes, plazas, gardens, and parks provide locales for necessary social bonding. Nature in the city often serves as a backdrop for courtship, political gatherings, criminal activity, family outings, athletic competition, and other forms of critical urban interaction. A study of fifty cemeteries in greater Boston found a variety of uses (Table 2), with 45 percent of cemetery visitors not involved in gravesite visits (Thomas and Dixon 1974).

Table 2.   Activities found in fifty greater Boston cemeteries during 200 hours of study

Activity	Total number of people
Family gravesite visits	726
Historic gravesite visits	657
Car drivers passing through	323
Pleasure walking	256
Relaxing or sleeping	218
Bicycling	104
Dog walking	40
Athletics, including baseball, football, golf, jogging, and Frisbee playing	35
Games, including chase tag, hide-and-seek, hopscotch, card playing, and setting off firecrackers	21
Drug or alcohol consumption, including glue sniffing and marijuana smoking	18
Feeding wildlife	18
Fishing	16
Berry picking	15
Chipmunk trapping	9
Stone rubbing	8
Gardening	6
Model plane flying	6
Photography	2
Drivers' education	2
Eating lunch	1
Car washing	1
Peeping Tom	1

Source: Thomas and Dixon (1974:108).

4. *There is a mixed pattern of ownership and access.* As Table 3 (Burch *et al.* 1978) suggests, there are several alternatives as to who owns natural areas within the city and who has access to them. The answers depend on cultural, political, economic, and historical circumstances.

Table 3.   A typology of urban ownership and access

	Private access	Public access
Private ownership	e.g., a person's residence	e.g., cemetery
Public ownership	e.g., a mayor's residence	e.g., public park

In feudal times, natural areas such as urban gardens and nearby hunting grounds were owned and managed by the lord, and the general population was barred from their use (Mumford 1956). The emergence of capitalism brought with it a redistribution of ownership and an increase in public access—the museum, amusement park, zoo, and aquarium took on the form of private property with regular public access. Contemporary parks, with public ownership and access, are more recent inventions; for example, New York's Central Park was developed in the 1850s.

The modern city shows a mixed pattern of ownership and access. Socioeconomic status tends to segregate neighborhoods and their residents, as Berry and Kasarda note:

> High-status neighborhoods typically are found in zones of superior residential amenity near water, trees, and higher ground, free from the risk of floods and away from smoke and factories, and increasingly in the furthest accessible peripheries. Middle-status neighborhoods press as close to the high-status ones as is feasible. To the low-status resident, least able to afford costs of commuting, are relinquished the least desirable areas adjacent to industrial zones radiating from the center of the city along railroads and rivers, the zones of highest pollution and the oldest, most deteriorated homes (1977:82).

Hence, access to urban nature may be related to a host of sociological and economic factors.

The most obvious natural areas are public-owned with public access (parks), but the amount of privately owned nature in the city may be surprisingly high. In the previously mentioned study of Boston cemeteries, 42 percent were privately owned, and 91 percent had public access. This is significant acreage, as over a third of Boston's open space is within its cemeteries (Thomas and Dixon 1974). Country clubs, yacht clubs, golf courses, and exclusive residential districts often include natural features. Ownership of urban nature may even be fashionable for corporations—the fringes of New York and its satellite cities are interspersed with company headquarters, each with acreage left in woodlot, glen, or open field.

Implications for Interpretation

It has been suggested that there are at least four characteristic patterns concerning nature in the city: minimal interdependence between the city and local nature, a tendency to collect and display exotica, the importance of nature as a backdrop for social integration, and mixed patterns of ownership and access. Each has implications for urban interpretation.

1. *The minimal interdependence with local nature makes urban interpretation more difficult.* Very few natural ecosystems exist in our large cities. While the Jamaica Bay Wildlife Refuge near New York's JFK Airport is an exception, Central Park's manicured setting is more typical. Most urban parks and preserves are in what ecologists call "anthropomorphic climax"; i.e., the community of plants and animals is dependent upon man's activities. Hence, local ecosystems are often altered, and it is difficult to find significant acreages that include native species in natural communities. Interpreting local nature may require extra effort to find, protect, and manage these places.

Further, the interdependence between an urban population and its "ghost acreage" is often disguised. Supermarkets serve as continuously stocked cornucopias, water is always on tap, and garbage is predictably carted off elsewhere (most of the time). In fact, it is not until natural disasters or social unrest (such as labor strikes) occur that these interdependencies are apparent to the urbanite. Interpreting a city's ghost acreage and its fragile ties to distant ecosystems could be an important revelation to urban populations.

2. *The city's role in collecting and displaying exotic nature is an opportunity and challenge.* As described earlier, the urban center is the locale for major botanical and zoological collections, both deliberate (zoos, arboretums, and aquariums) and circumstantial (residential landscaping, maintained ball fields, vacant lots, and so forth). Such exotic flora and fauna play important roles in the anthropomorphic climax communities of most urban open space. Interpretive efforts could focus on the utilitarian values of nature in the city—the approach largely taken by those involved in urban forestry programs (Driver *et al.* 1978).

Nature interpretation in an urban society competes with the other attractions of the city. Art museums, theaters, movie houses, concert halls, and sport stadiums are all examples of the urban center's ability to concentrate and mix the human and economic resources of a region. While several studies have found environmental concerns and park-going associated with high levels of education and income (Cheek and Burch 1976), other cultural institutions draw similar audiences. An opportunity lies in creatively linking interpretive programs with special exhibits in art galleries, with concert series, and even with sporting events.

Urban exhibits of nature attract a nonlocal audience, and this special population may present special challenges. For example, visitors to zoos and aquariums may include a substantial number of vacationing families, suburbanites and foreign tourists (Cheek 1976). Research by Berry and Kasarda (1977) documents that suburban populations in general, and the commuting population in particular, have large impacts on urban recreational services already strained by lack of financial resources. They note:

> Exacerbating the service-resource problem facing the central cities has been the fact that suburban population growth has not been matched by a proportional growth of suburban public services . . . Evidently, it is not economically rational for suburban-area residents to build and operate their own libraries, large parks, zoos, museums, or other public facilities if they have ready and free access to those in the central city (1977:226).

A key challenge to urban interpretation is to increase the role of suburbs in providing interpretive opportunities or contributing to the cities' efforts.

Further, nonlocal audiences may require special interpretive programming. Interpretive planning for distinct populations is important (Machlis and Field 1974), and nonlocal visitors are no exception. They may require more information concerning visitor services and regulations and an interpretive introduction to the city as a whole. The opportunity is to reach a regional, national, and international audience with introductory programs that may also prove popular with locals.

3. *Because urban nature is a setting for critical forms of social integration, interpreters should plan for each activity.* The gardens, riverfronts, parks, and zoos of our major cities also are settings for strengthening the social bonds of kinship, friendship, and neighborhood. Urban interpretive programs can offer these social values at the same time they inform and inspire visitors. In a study of an urban park in China, Machlis *et al.* found this multipurpose use of urban nature to be widespread:

> Just as a particular location in the park can be used for many purposes at the same time, a particular activity can serve several park functions. An example is the raising of lotus (*Nelumbo nucifera*). The flower is enjoyed for its aesthetic value during the Lotus Blossom Festival, which brings together people from throughout the region. The petals are a culinary delicacy. Leaves of the plant are used in cooking to wrap food stuffs. The young root of the lotus is slivered and eaten; older roots of the plant are milled into flour. Thus, one activity within the park serves many purposes (1981:10).

Natural areas may be important locales for holding festivals, craft fairs, exhibitions, and other large-group activities. Natural history programs may be organized to maximize the social bonding of smaller groups—e.g., interpretation that encourages parent-child interaction.

The social processes that characterize urban open space may also have negative consequences. Competition between interpretive programs and other uses may range from the commonplace (joggers versus birdwatchers) to extreme cases of conflict and displacement, such as juvenile gangs coopting territory for their operations. These managerial realities will affect urban interpretation.

4. *The mixed pattern of public and private property ownership will require cooperation between the public and private
sectors.* In the previous section, I described how postfeudal econo-
mies led to a mixed pattern of public and private property ownership and access, and how speculation and development acted to
reduce the amount of urban open space.

What is preserved are likely to be fragments of ecosystems,
though certain city parks closely resemble whole ecological units
(e.g., Rock Creek Park is an important watershed in Washington,
D.C.). Interpretive programs that effectively deal with the levels of
community and ecosystem must usually cross boundaries between
public and private rights. For example, few urban waterfronts
could be interpreted well without encountering almost every type
of ownership/access pattern described in Table 3.

Hence, cooperation between the public and private sectors
may be a necessity for effective urban interpretation. Opportunities for such cooperation exist; the recently completed National
Urban Recreation Study found that 70 percent of the neighborhoods surveyed had private nonprofit recreational services, and
44 percent had private for-profit services. Further, Table 4 shows
these services are often located in residential districts away from
large urban parks. Interpretive programs could be integrated into
these agencies' and businesses' traditional programming.

Table 4.   Percentage of urban neighborhoods with private nonprofit recreation services

Neighborhood income level	Percentage
High	50
Medium	67
Low	80

Source: Heritage, Conservation and Recreation Service (1980).

Interpretation in an Urban Society

Clearly, the possibilities for urban nature interpretation are as
varied as the potential sources of environmental knowledge in the
city. In addition to the traditional interpretive efforts at large
parks, zoos, and aquariums, many other types of institutions are
involved: factories and light industries give tours; breweries are
open to beer-tasting visitors; travel companies offer ferry rides,

bus rides, and walking tours; and so forth. *All have potential as part of an urban interpretation program.*

Further support comes from the study of tourism. In his book *The Tourist: A New Theory of the Leisure Class,* Dean MacCannell (1976) suggests that much of the way we interpret new environments is structurally similar to the processes used by tourists. His analysis of urban touristic activity argues for a wider view of urban interpretation. MacCannell suggests that for tourists, urban areas are composed of tourist districts: Paris is made up of the Latin Quarter, Pigalle, and Montparnasse; San Francisco is made up of Haight-Ashbury, the Barbary Coast, and Chinatown. Tour guides and travel literature suggest or recommend certain regions, communities and neighborhoods, and the tourist then "discovers" such features as markets, restaurants, people, and importantly, nature.

Several features seem to be especially attractive as objects of tourist interpretation: commercial establishments, special residential districts, unique occupations and public works (including parks). A striking example is the famous tour of the Paris sewer system. A guidebook published in 1900 describes the tour:

> In the Place du Chatelet is one of the novel entrances to the vast network of sewers by which Paris is undermined. They are generally shown to the public on the second and fourth Wednesday of each month in the summer . . . The visit, in which ladies need have no hesitation in taking part, lasts about 1 hour, and ends at the Place de la Madeleine. Visitors are conveyed partly on comfortable electric cars, partly in boats, so that no fatigue is involved (Baedeker 1900:64).

What is arresting about this example is its potential for interpreting the urban environment. All components of the city, no matter how unrelated they are on the surface, are interconnected underground. This is interpretation at its ecological best, and it is fascinating for the urban dweller and visitor alike. We interpreters need to develop similar activities; I believe this to be the challenge of interpretation in an urban society.

Some Radical Comments on Interpretation: A Little Heresy is Good for the Soul

Kenneth L. Nyberg

"Do not say, 'Draw the curtain that I may see the painting.' The curtain is the painting."
Nikos Kazantzakis

IN ONE OF the more pretentious descriptions of environmental interpretation, Carr (1976) is reputed to have said that:

> . . . not having an interpreter in a park is like inviting a guest to your house, opening the door, and then disappearing.

Unlike Carr, I rather suspect that not having an interpreter in a park is more like returning to your own home and not having a salesman there waiting for you. Indeed, it is the essential thrust of my thesis that environmental interpretation is not only largely unnecessary, but significantly more likely to produce harm than benefit.

There is a considerable body of literature addressed to modes and means of improving environmental interpretation. What is not considered is the fundamental character of the phenomenon itself—i.e., the more radical questions of "what is it, why is it, and what has accrued because of it?" As a beginning, I offer three short answers to these three short questions. The remainder of this essay will elaborate these considerations.

Adapted from "Some Radical Comments on Interpretation," by Kenneth L. Nyberg. (Paper presented at the Annual Workshop of the Association of Interpretive Naturalists, College Station, Texas, April 7, 1977).

Regarding the first of these questions—what is environmental interpretation?—it appears that the interpreter does three things: (1) the interpreter tells the audience what it already knows, or (2) the interpreter tells the audience what it does not want to know, or (3) the interpreter tells the audience more or less than it should know. The important thing to remember here is that the interpreter is forever "telling" the environment to others.

The second question—why environmental interpretation?—is even simpler to answer. Having considered the question of why we have interpreters at all, I have come to the only conclusion possible: that the interpreter exists as a service to the good Bishop Berkeley, so that if a tree should fall in the forest we can be sure that it does make a sound, because someone is in fact there to hear it.

The third question—what hath environmental interpretation wrought?—is considerably more complicated but can generally be answered by noting the plaques on every conceivable house. The interpreter, much like Lot, continues to glance over his shoulder just in time to see everything turning to salt. Before him lies plague, pestilence, and immeasurable debauchery in the cathedral.

There is something wholly audacious about the environmental interpreter's work. Much like the doorman treating the landlord as a tenant—and an undesirable one at that—the interpreter is involved in convincing the public that their land is in fact his, and if they are good they may visit it for a short period of time. The term for this in Yiddish is "chutzpah," which basically means "unmitigated gall." Not only is such gall unmitigated, but it is also undiminished. Having convinced the owner that he is not the owner, and having provided him with a new title ("visitor"), the interpreter than proceeds to convince him that he is ignorant, as well. The visitor does not see, taste, hear, feel, or smell what he sees, tastes, hears, feels or smells. Rather, he *mis*-sees, tastes, hears, feels and smells what is "really" there. Hence, the visitor does not see a pretty, leafy tree sprouting nutlike growth, nor does he even see the "Ohio Buckeye." Rather, the visitor misperceives what is, in fact, an *Aesculus glabra.*

In short, the environmental interpreter is in the business of "telling" reality, thus denying to all others present the inspiration of speculation. To remove, hinder, or displace this speculation is to destroy reality; borrowing from T. S. Eliot (1952:117), reality is:

> An abstraction
> Remaining a perpetual possibility
> Only in a world of speculation

and by telling it, no longer is the possibility possible. Telling reality negates reality and ultimately negates man himself. As the philosopher Heidegger (1961) notes, the fundament of man is brought forth in a threefold act of founding a world (*Grunden*), discovering the things-that-are (*Shiften*), and endowing them with a sense or meaning (*ontologische, Begrunden des Seienden*). The interpreter, by telling a meaning, diminishes discovery and ultimately precludes man's founding of a world.

Realities are nothing more than ways of knowing, things to be known. When the interpreter tells his reality, he does not share it on an equal footing. Rather, he tells it so that it now is to be someone else's reality. It is an act of epistemological violence, not simply saying "my reality is better than your reality," but "my reality *is* reality." All else is illusion or delusion.

Much like the priest who observed that it is almost impossible to have a religious experience during a church service, I am compelled to argue that an environmental experience is far more often precluded by interpretive programs than facilitated. Indeed, it has always struck me much like programmed love-making, complete with a coach. Whatever technical knowledge the coach can provide will hardly compensate for the loss of passion and intimacy. It is damnably difficult to enjoy what you are doing when some other person keeps shouting instructions.

Aside from meeting the quizzical demands of Berkeley's dilemma, the very real question remains; why environmental interpretive programs in the first place? It is important to remember that, unlike the proverbial chicken and egg, the interpreter clearly did not precede either the environment or the actor in it. And, improbable as it may seem, far more people have benefited from an uninterpreted river than from an interpreted one. If God had wished for there to be interpretive programs He or She would have properly labeled trees and rock formations in the first place.

Essentially, interpretation—the telling activity—was largely instituted to *provide* a need, not to meet one. Prior to interpretive programming, such responsibility was entrusted to various incompetents such as fathers, mothers, friends, or—worst of all—one's own imagination and scholarship. This occasionally led to such crises of consciousness and faith as confusing a douglas fir with a slash pine, sandstone for limestone, and the yellow-bellied sapsucker with the loon. Such *angst* was relieved by the presence of the interpreter. Now one did not have to make up something when one didn't know, or figure it out for oneself; someone was present to assume this responsibility. Not only could we now be sure that the tree is, in fact, a douglas fir, but we also were immeasurably enhanced—interpretive programs invariably enhance—by the knowledge that the average twelve-year-old douglas fir regenerates 11,156 needles every year, while the loon hardly any.

I do not mean to deny the fact that a great many people like interpretive programs; they prefer having their world told to them. Generally, however, people who like interpretive programs also believe the Northwest Passage was opened by Coleman and Winnebago. Their idea of a primitive campsite is one where the television reception is bad and the ice machine is at least 30 yards away.

The argument goes that we need interpretive programming to meet the increasing demand of visitor populations. One of the reasons for this increasing visitor population is greater numbers of interpretive programs. My suggestion is to cut off the snake's head and let the body die. Simply abandon every interpretive program; tear up every access road; dismantle every prepared campsite and refreshment stand; and remove every plaque, sign, poster, arrow, and restroom. What will occur? Basically, fewer people will attend parks, wilderness areas, and forests. Only those people truly interested will go, not as visitors but rather as indigents. After all, where is it written that everyone needs a wilderness experience, properly interpreted or not?

If you can imagine the consequences of my suggestion, then you know the "what," "why" and "benefit" of interpretive programming: pure Keynesian economics. Indeed, the only unquestioned benefit of interpretive programming is that it:

> May assist in the successful promotion of parks where tourism is essential to an area's. . . economy (Sharpe 1976:9).

In this regard, the intepreter becomes a lackey for the exploitive interests of the bourgeois, and—unless pay scales have improved immeasurably—like all lackeys, does not participate in the bourgeois' profits.

Do I truly view interpretive programming as encouraging Bad Faith (Sartre 1957), playing *reductio absurdum* with the natural environment, and unwittingly participating in capitalist exploitation? The answer is yes. A student and—until now, at least—a good friend, has argued that the interpreter should ". . . assume a role that supports public mental health services" (Philipp 1976:12). I take this suggestion as final evidence that I am right. Interpreters perceive their role far too ambitiously. It is not simply outrageous, it is dangerous as well. They tamper with the lives—mental, physical and spiritual—of people. Interpreters take from people not only their definitions but their defining capabilities and processes too. Interpretation has moved from prophecy to priesthood; interpreters' proclamations no longer are prayer, but revelation. And the fundamental question is: do they know what they are doing?

By now, I suspect I read like Madalyn Murray O'Hare at the Southern Baptist Convention. In truth, my remarks are intended to challenge complacency. I believe it is useful to question the very basis of that which we do—to go to the roots, to be radical. This is true of science, life, and interpretive programming, as well. Quite often the journey itself is more important than the ultimate destination. Quoting one of James Agee's (1960:458) wonderful aphorisms, "the tigers of wrath are wiser than the horses of instruction," Zaner goes on to observe that:

> One learns little or nothing if he avoids the central tigers of his discipline or craft, even though remaining with the gentle, domesti-

cated horses may seem safer. It is necessary, then, to enter the fray; not for me to pretend to instruct, which is for horses, but rather to take up the issues directly, inviting you to think through with me the sense of criticism and its demands on thinking (1970:178).

It is my hope that this essay serves as a catalyst for such a demand on thinking, and that interpreters devote time to the critical consideration of environmental interpretation: what is it, why is it, and what has accrued because of it? We need to confront the tigers—if only to grab them by the tail—and consider seriously this topic which I have only poorly delineated.

CONCLUSION

In this book we have tried to establish a foundation for the utilization of sociology in support of interpretation. We have done so in a restrictive fashion—by drawing attention to the diversity of people who utilize interpretive services. Our approach has been illustrative rather than exhaustive, in part because our knowledge about people is limited and the manner in which sociology can be applied to interpretation is still emerging. We have essentially argued that by understanding the behavior of specific visitor populations, communication of interpretive messages will be enhanced. Implied throughout was the principle that alternative forms of interpretation should be employed—not simply because they are unique or new—but because they are appropriate to a particular visitor public.

We recognize that only a piece of the puzzle has been explored. Interpreters must expand their attention even more—to the managerial realities of budgets, politics, communication technologies, and so forth. Social scientists interested in interpretation may need to consider new research perspectives that can deal with the political, social, economic, and environmental contexts within which interpretation takes place. What new approaches might be useful? We offer one suggestion—the application of human ecology to interpretation.

Human Ecology and Interpretation

The essence of human ecology is a recognition of *Homo sapiens* as part of the ecosystem, an integral part of nature (Machlis *et al.* 1981). Relative to other disciplinary orientations, the human ecological approach to interpretation emphasizes a broad set of variables and relationships. Its central concept, the *human ecosystem,* is defined by the interaction of people, social organization, and available technology in response to a set of environmental conditions. Interpretive settings such as national parks or urban historic sites could be considered as human ecosystems. Created by society, these natural and cultural entities reflect a social organization and technology for the preservation and use of unique resources. A state or regional museum, an aquarium, an art center, or a zoo can be treated as a complex system with daily flows of people, information, energy, materials, and so forth.

Human ecosystems are dynamic and adaptive; i.e., the feedback mechanisms linking human populations to resources can change over time. For example, moving an interpretive program to a new location or time may require visitors to change their schedules, alter density levels in a visitor center, increase impacts on one resource and lessen those on another, and force interpreters and maintenance crews to adapt their work operations and home life. "Adaptation" is a crucial term here. John Bennett, the anthropologist, writes:

> Adaptive behavior is viewed as multidimensional: what may be adaptive for one individual is maladaptive for another or for the group; what may be adaptive for humans may not be so for Nature (1976:3).

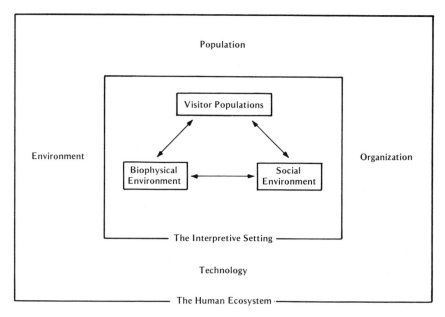

Figure 1.   Human ecological view of interpretive settings.

Figure 1 presents this human ecological view of interpretive settings. The *biophysical environment* represents those resources set aside as vignettes of natural or cultural history that support the human activity within a park or other locale. For example, a river may function as a natural area for hiking, a setting for historical interpretation, and as a source of potable water for park staff and visitors. The *social environment* includes the formal organizations that affect interpretive activities, such as the management agency, concessionaires, natural history associations, special interest groups, and so forth. It also includes the prevalent norms for behavior—i.e., the social definitions of which activities are appropriate within the setting.

In the human ecological perspective, visitors are a key population. Writing about national parks, Campbell notes:

> . . . Humans are the dominant species in every National Park. As a result of our social evolution we have expanded into one niche after another. We have created new niches where none existed. Further, we are a highly generalized animal, capable of an immense range of behaviors ... In short, to understand the natural systems of the park you must understand the park's most dominant species (1979:53).

Visitor publics vary in their cultural content and expression; as this volume has shown, they represent diverse subpopulations. The interrelationship of these diverse visitor groups and a complex setting like a park or historic site requires substantial adaptation. An interpretive program that describes local flora, fauna, and history, informs visitors as to hiking and sightseeing opportunities, and explains park regulations is part of this adaptive process. Seen in this light, interpretation is an exchange of information critical to adaptation within a park ecosystem, and the interpreter fulfills a very real ecological function.

Hence, the human ecological framework has several advantages. It is broad in scope and considers several variables not yet widely explored in interpretation research. It is dynamic in its concern with the everchanging process of adaptation within the interpretive setting. Interpretation is treated as an ecological function, linked to other park activities and critical to park management. Lastly, this approach may help stimulate a new set of research questions regarding interpretation.

Avenues for Future Research

A human ecological approach to interpretation suggests several avenues for future research.

Adaptive Strategies as Explanations of Behavior

The human ecological framework places interpretation in the center of certain adaptive strategies for coping with park environments. Earlier in this book, Machlis found that single-parent families often attended interpretive programs in order to gain needed information on other park activities; extended families familiar with a park had no such inclination. Similarly, the behavior of foreign tourists in U.S. parks may be linked to the kinds of interpretive programs they receive. Here, adaptive behavior could be measured with a variety of indicators—accident records, violations, souvenir expenditures, interpretive contacts, and so forth. Time-budget studies which attempt to compare visitors' time spent on interpretive activities versus sustenance, shelter, and other basic behaviors may also be instructive.

The Impact of Institutional Relations on Interpretation

Our framework implies that interpretation is not isolated from other activities within a park, nor is it limited to the organizations responsible for park management. At Grand Canyon National Park, interpretation is carried out by transportation companies (airlines provide guided tours, leaflets, and other materials), by concessionaires (a small museum at one hotel), by private tour companies (including European firms) and by the National Park Service. Certainly, the institutional relations between these organizations may help predict the kinds of interpretation that visitors experience.

Further, external organizations may affect interpretation by influencing the distribution of visitors over space and time. Airline schedules and highway access routes may determine length of stay; the economics of mass tourism may determine size of group, and the travel industry may concentrate its advance bookings into predictable peak seasons. Ecological studies of this sort may greatly improve interpretive planning and effectiveness.

Interpretation as an Agent of Social Change

Interpretation may be linked to a variety of sociological variables, including social norms. Hence, interpretation can be proposed as an agent of social change that in turn could lead to ecological change. Research is necessary to explore how (or if) interpretation affects the norms and behaviors of visitors who experience it, and if these effects have consequences for the human ecosystem.

An example is energy interpretation. Interpretive programs may alter visitors' views on energy development (a normative change) and require resource agencies like the National Park Service and Department of Energy to cooperate on programs (an institutional change). They may increase conservation activities (a behavioral change), which reduce energy demand (an ecological change). For these kinds of studies, the sociological literature on adoption and diffusion of innovations may be helpful.

The Continued Diversity of Visitor Groups

The diversity of visitor groups is likely to grow as America becomes more multiethnic and multicultural. In this book, we have examined children, families, seniors, foreign tourists, and cruise ship travelers. But what of spelunkers, hang-gliding enthusiasts, anglers, and other outdoor recreation enthusiasts? Are there important differences for interpreters between the rich, the poor, and the middle class? Do German or British tourists have different interpretive needs than the Japanese or Saudis? Are visitors from the older, industrialized North Atlantic and New England states different than those from the developing Rocky Mountain and Southwestern states?

These questions require careful, descriptive case studies. Such studies could focus on the ecological question of adaptation: how does a specific visitor group adapt to the interpretive setting, and what are the consequences for the visitor, the resource, and the interpreter? As the number of case studies increases, our ecological understanding of people and parks should be enriched.

Public vs. Private-Sector Interpretation

The management of parks, historic sites, and other recreation areas is predominantly the management of human services—from sewer systems to employee payrolls. The evolution and expansion of such activities has tended to highlight a critical debate—who should provide such services? Our economic system, as a mixture of capitalism and government intervention, provides three major alternatives: the public sector, the private sector, or some combination of the two.

Parks and historic areas, as part of our culture and economy, are not immune from this debate. Specifically for interpretation, what is the optimum mix of public and private-sector interpretive services? While this question is obviously a policy matter, research is needed to find appropriate alternatives. Analyses of operation costs, agency subsidies, competition, supply, demand, and willingness to pay for interpretive experiences might aid policymakers in deciding appropriate roles for public and private-sector interpretive services.

Changes in the Interpretive Work Force

As Johnson and Field pointed out in their essay, the American population is changing, and such change has broad implications for managers of natural and human resources. Of particular interest is the impact that demographic change will have on the interpretive work force. Who will be the interpreters and naturalists of the 1990s? How and where will they be educated and trained? What skills will be essential?

In addition, the management of interpretive services deserves analysis. What organizational forms are most productive? Are there administrative strategies, such as job-sharing and "flextime," that might be beneficial to interpreters? How might the interpretive profession adapt to the rise of volunteerism?

The human ecological perspective, by focusing on the interdependencies of people, society, and the environment, may provide a useful framework for dealing with such critical topics. Research is now being conducted by social scientists on many of these issues; a new synthesis based on ecological principles seems plausible in the near future. Perhaps another volume on interpretation will be appropriate.

The Future

In his book *MegaTrends,* John Naisbitt describes the 1980s as a special and ambivalent decade. He writes:

We are living in the *time of the parenthesis,* the time between eras. It is as though we have bracketed off the present from both the past and the future, for we are neither here nor there. We have not quite left behind the either/or America of the past—centralized, industrialized and economically self-contained ...

But we have not embraced the future either. We have done the human thing: we are clinging to the known past in fear of the unknown future . . . those who are willing to handle the ambiguity of this in-between period and to anticipate the new era will be a quantum leap ahead of those who hold on to the past. The time of the parenthesis is a time of change and questioning (1982:249).

The result is that the 1980s are an exciting period to be an interpreter of natural and cultural history. New technologies, budget priorities, cultural values, and audiences require interpreters to seek useful knowledge wherever they may find it. We hope that sociology can be part of that useful knowledge. All might remember Freeman Tilden's admonition in *The Fifth Essence:*

Interpretation is a voyage of discovery in the field of human emotions and intellectual growth, and it is hard to foresee that time when the interpreter can confidently say, *"Now* we are wholly adequate to our task" (n.d.).

REFERENCES CITED

Agee, J. 1960. *Let us now praise famous men.* Boston: Houghton-Mifflin.

Anderson, N. 1923. *The hobo.* Chicago: University of Chicago Press.

Baedeker, K. 1900. *Paris and environs.* 14th rev. ed. Leipzik: Baedeker Publishers.

Bane, M. J.; and Weiss, R. S. 1980. Alone together—the world of single parent families. *American Demographics* 2(5):11-15.

Bassard, J.; and Boll, E. 1950. *Ritual in family living: a contemporary study.* Philadelphia: University of Philadelphia.

Bennett, J. W. 1976. *The ecological transition: Cultural anthropology and human adaptation.* New York: Pergamon Press.

Berger, P. L.; and Kellner, H. 1981. *Sociology reinterpreted.* Garden City, NJ: Doubleday.

Berry, B.; and Kasarda, J. 1977. *Contemporary urban ecology.* New York: MacMillan.

Blood, R. W.; and Wolfe, P. M. 1971. Resources and family task performance. In *Sociology of the family,* ed. M. Anderson. Baltimore: Penguin Books.

Bolyard, J. E. 1981. International travel and passenger fares, 1980. *Survey of Current Business* 61(5):29-34.

Buck, R. C. 1978. Boundary maintenance revisited: tourist experience in an old order Amish community. *Rural Sociology* 43(2):221-234.

Bultena, G.; Field, D. R.; and Renninger, R. 1977. Interpretation for the elderly: a study of the interpretive interests of retired national parkgoers. *Journal of Interpretation* 3(2):29-32.

Burch, W. R. 1964. The play world of camping. *American Journal of Sociology* 48:604-612.

Burch, W. R. 1971. *Daydreams and nightmares: A sociological essay on the American environment.* New York: Harper & Row.

Burch, W. R., Jr. 1974. Observation as a technique for recreation research. In *Land and leisure: Concepts and methods in outdoor recreation,* ed. C. Van Doren. Chicago: Maaroufa Press.

Burch, W. R.; and Wenger, W., Jr. 1967. *The social characteristics of participants in three styles of family camping.* USDA Forest Service Gen. Tech. Rep. PNW-48. Portland, Or: Pacific Northwest Forest and Range Experiment Station.

Burch, W. R., Jr.; DeLuca, D.; Machlis, G. E.; Burch-Minakan, L.; and Zimmerman, C. 1978. *Handbook for assessing energy-society relations.* Washington, D.C.: U.S. Department of Energy Report, Office of Inexhaustible Resources.

Burgess, E. W.; Locke, H. J.; and Thomes, M. 1971. *The family.* New York: Van Nostrand Reinhold.

Campbell, A. 1981. *The sense of well being in America: Recent patterns and trends.* New York: McGraw-Hill.

Campbell, C. A. 1974. Survival of reptiles and amphibians in urban environments. In *Symposium on wildlife in an urbanizing environment,* Planning and Resources Development Series #28. Amherst, MA: Cooperative Extension Service.

Campbell, F. L. 1970. Participant observation in outdoor recreation. *Journal of Leisure Research* 2(4):226-236.

Campbell, F. L. 1979. The edge effect: Life in the ecotone. (Paper presented at the Second Conference on Scientific Research in the National Parks, San Francisco, California.)

Carr, W. H. 1976. Uncited quote In *Interpreting the environment,* ed. G. W. Sharpe. New York: John Wiley and Sons.

Catton, W. R., Jr. 1980. *Overshoot: the ecological basis of revolutionary change.* Chicago: University of Illinois Press.

Cheek, N. H., Jr. 1971a. Intragroup social structure and social solidarity in park settings (Paper presented at the American Association for the Advancement of Science Symposium, Philadelphia, Pennsylvania, December 26-31, 1971).

Cheek, N. H., Jr. 1971b. Toward a sociology of non work. *Pacific Sociological Review* 14(July):245-259.

Cheek, N. H., Jr. 1972. Variations in patterns of leisure behavior: An analysis of sociological aggregates. In *Social behavior, natural resources, and the environment,* ed. W. R. Burch, Jr., N. H. Cheek, Jr., and L. Taylor, 23-29. New York: Harper & Row.

Cheek, N. H., Jr. 1976. Sociological perspectives on the zoological park. In *Leisure and recreation places,* ed. N. H. Cheek, Jr., D. R. Field, and R. J. Burdge. Ann Arbor: Ann Arbor Science.

Cheek, N. H., Jr.; and Burch, W. R., Jr. 1976. *The social organization of leisure in human society.* New York: Harper and Row.

Cheek, N. H., Jr.; and Field, D. R. 1971. *North Pacific border study.* Seattle: University of Washington College of Forest Resources.

Clark, R. N. 1976. *How to control litter in recreation areas: The incentive system.* USDA Forest Service Gen. Tech. Rep. Portland, OR: Pacific Northwest Forest and Range Experiment Station.

Clark, R. N.; Burgess, R. L.; and Hendee, J. C. 1972a. The development of anti-litter behavior in a forest campground. *Journal of Applied Behavior Analysis* 5(Spring):1-5.

Clark, R. N.; Hendee, J. C.; and Burgess, R. L. 1972b. The experimental control of littering. *Journal of Environmental Education* 4(2):22-28.

Clark, R. N.; Hendee, J. C.; and Campbell, F. L. 1971. Values, behavior, and conflict in modern camping culture. *Journal of Leisure Research* 3(Summer):143-159.

Clark, R. N.; and Lucas, R. C. 1978. *The forest ecosystem of Southeast Alaska: Outdoor recreation and scenic resources.* USDA Forest Service Gen. Tech. Rep. PNW-66. Portland, OR: Pacific Northwest Forest and Range Experiment Station.

Clawson, M. and Knetsch, J. L. 1966. *Economics of outdoor recreation*. Baltimore: John Hopkins Press.

Cleaver, E. 1970. The land question and black liberation. In *What country have I? Political writings by black Americans,* ed. H. J. String. New York: St. Martin's Press.

Crider, D. M.; Willits, F. K.; and Bealer, F. C. 1973. Panel studies: some practical problems. *Sociological Methods* 2(1):3-19.

Data Resources, Inc. 1981. Demographic forecast: Family size. *American Demographics* 3(1):50-51.

Data Resources, Inc. 1982. Demographic forecast: Baby boom families. *American Demographics* 4(4):46-47.

Dean, J. P.; Eichhorn, R. L.; and Dean, L. R. 1969. Limitations and advantages of unstructured methods. In *Issues in participant observation: A text and reader,* ed. G. J. McCall and J. L. Simmons, 19-24. Chicago: Addison-Wesley.

Deloria, V., Jr. 1969. *Custer died for your sins*. New York: MacMillan.

Deutscher, I. 1966. Words and deeds: Social science and social policy. *Sociological Problems* 13:235-254.

Dotson, F. 1951. Patterns of voluntary association among urban working-class families. *American Sociological Review* 16:689-693.

Driver, B. L.; Rosenthal, D.; and Peterson, G. 1979. Social benefits of urban forests and related green spaces in cities. In *Proceedings of national urban forestry conference,* ed. G. Hopkins. Syracuse: State University of New York, College of Environmental Science and Forestry.

Dulles, F. R. 1965. *A history of recreation: America learns to play*. New York: Meredith Publishers.

Duncan, O. D.; Schuman, H.; and Duncan, B. 1973. *Social change in a metropolitan community*. New York: Russell Sage.

Dunn, D. R. 1980. Urban recreation research: an overview. *Leisure Sciences* 3:(1):25-27.

Durkheim, E. 1947. *The division of labor in society*. New York: Free Press.

Dwyer, J. F.; O'Leary, J. T.; and Theobald, W. F. 1979. Putting the cart before the horse: When does the data catch up to the theory? (Paper presented at the Tourism and the Next Decade International Symposium, George Washington University, Washington, D.C.).

Eliot, T. S. 1952. *The complete poems and plays, 1909-1950*. New York: Harcourt Brace.

Field, D. R. 1971. Interchangeability of parks with other leisure settings. (Paper presented at the AAAS Symposium, Philadelphia, Pennsylvania, December 26-31, 1971).

Field, D. R. 1972. Visitors to parks in the Pacific Northwest. (Paper presented at the Pacific Northwest Region Superintendents' Conference, Portland, Oregon, March 16-18, 1972).

Field, D. R. and Wagar, J. A. 1973. Visitor groups and interpretation in parks and other outdoor leisure settings. *Journal of Environmental Education* 5(1):12-17.

Freeman, R. B. 1979. The work force of the future: An overview. In *Work in America the decade ahead,* Ed. K. Clark and J. Rosow. New York: Van Nostrand Reinhold.

Freund, J. 1968. *The sociology of Max Weber.* Trans. M. Ilford. New York: Pantheon Books.

Geismar, L. L. 1964. Family functioning as an index of need for welfare services. *Family Process* 3(2):99-111.

Gold, R. L. 1958. Roles in sociological field observations. *Social Forces* 36(3): 217-233.

Graves, P. F. 1972. Summation of the forest recreation symposium. In *Summary of the forest recreation symposium,* 12-21. Forest Service Research Paper NE-235. Upper Darby, PA: Northeast Forest and Range Experiment Station.

Hancock, H. K. 1973. Recreation preference: Its relation to user behavior. *Journal of Forestry* 71(6):336-337.

Hawley, A. H. 1971. *Urban society: An ecological approach.* New York: Ronald Press.

Hayghe, H. 1981. Two income families. *American Demographics* 3(8):35-39.

Heberlein, T. A. 1971. Moral norms, threatened sanctions, and littering behavior. Ph.D. diss. University of Wisconsin.

Heberlein, T. A. 1973. Social psychological assumptions of user attitude surveys: The case of the wilderness scale. *Journal of Leisure Research* 5(3):18-33.

Heidegger, M. 1961. *Being and time.* Trans., J. Macquarrie and E. Robinson. New York: Harper and Row.

Hendee, J. C. 1972a. Challenging the folklore of environmental education. *The Journal of Environmental Education* 3(3):19-23.

Hendee, J. C. 1972b. No, to attitudes to evaluate environmental education. *Journal of Environmental Education* 3(3).

Hendee, J. C.; Gale, R. P.; and Catton, W. R., Jr. 1971. A typology of outdoor recreation activity preferences. *Journal of Leisure Research* 3(1).

Heritage, Conservation and Recreation Service. 1980. *National urban recreation study.* Washington, D.C.: Government Printing Office.

Hess, R.; and Handel, G. 1974. *Family worlds: A psychosocial approach to family life.* Chicago: University of Chicago Press.

Hobbs, D. A.; and Blank, S. J. 1982. *Sociology and the human experience,* 3rd ed. New York: John Wiley & Sons.

Howard, W. E. 1974. Why wildlife in an urban society? In *Symposium on wildlife in an urbanizing environment.* Planning and Resources Development Series #28. Amherst: Massachusetts Cooperative Extension Service.

Hughes, J. D. 1975. *Ecology in ancient civilizations.* Albuquerque: University of New Mexico Press.

Jackson, G.; Masnick, G.; Bulton, R.; Barlett, S.; and Pitkin, J. 1981. *Regional diversity and growth in the United States 1960-1990.* Boston: Auburn House Publishing.

Japanese National Tourist Organization. 1979. *Tourism in Japan 1978.* Tokyo: Department of Tourism, Ministry of Transport.

Japanese National Tourist Organization. 1981. *Tourism in Japan 1980.* Tokyo: Department of Tourism, Ministry of Transport.

Kazantzakis, N. 1960. *The saviors of God.* New York: Simon and Schuster.

Keep America Beautiful. 1968. *Who litters and why: Results of a survey of public awareness and concern about the problem of litter.* New York: Keep America Beautiful.

Kerlinger, F. N. 1973. *Foundations of behavioral research.* New York: Holt, Rinehart and Winston.

Lebra, J. S. 1976. *Japanese patterns of behavior.* Honolulu: University Press of Hawaii.

Lee, R. G. 1972. The social definition of outdoor recreation places. In *Social behavior, natural resources and the environment,* ed. W. R. Burch, Jr., N. H. Cheek, Jr., and L. Taylor. New York: Harper and Row.

Leibow, E. 1976. *Tally's corner.* Boston: Little, Brown & Co.

Lewis, C. S. 1969. On three ways of writing for children. In *Only connect: Readings on children's literature,* ed. S. Egoff, G. T. Stubbs, and L. F. Ashley, 207-220. New York: Oxford University Press.

Lime, D. W.; and Lorence, G. A. 1974. *Improving estimates of wilderness use from mandatory travel permits.* USDA Forest Service Research Paper NC-101. St. Paul, MN: North Central Forest and Range Experiment Station.

Linhart, S. 1975. The use and meaning of leisure in present-day Japan. In *Modern Japan,* ed. W. G. Beasley. Berkeley: University of California Press.

Litwak, E. 1960. Occupational mobility and extended family cohesion. *American Sociology Review* 25:9-21.

Litwak, E. 1961. Voluntary associations and neighborhood cohesion. *American Sociology Review* 26:258-71.

MacCannell, D. 1976. *The tourist: A new theory of the leisure class.* New York: Schocken Books.

Machlis, G. E. 1975. Families in parks: An analysis of family organization in a leisure setting. Master's thesis, University of Washington, Seattle.

Machlis, G. E.; and Field, D. R. 1974. Getting connected: an approach to children's interpretation. *Trends* 7:19-25.

Machlis, G. E.; Field, D. R.; and Campbell, F. L. 1981. The human ecology of parks. *Leisure Sciences* 4(3):195-212.

Machlis, G. E.; McLaughlin, W. J.; and Yu-Lian, Liu. 1981. An urban park in China: Xuan Wu Hu. *Parks and Recreation* 16:(8):20-29.

Mager, R. F. 1962. *Preparing instructional objectives.* Belmont, CA: Fearon Publishers.

Martindale, D. 1960. *American society.* Princeton: D. Van Nostrand.

Marx, L. 1964. *The machine in the garden: technology and the pastoral ideal in America.* London: Oxford University Press.

Mead, M. 1964. Anthropology and the camera. In *Encyclopedia of photography,* 166-181. New York: Graystone Press.

Melko, M.; and Cargan, L. 1981. The singles boom. *American Demographics* 3(10):30-31.

Michelson, W. 1976. *Man and his urban environment.* Reading, MA: Addison-Wesley.

Mumford, L. 1956. The natural history of urbanization. In *Man's role in changing the face of the earth,* ed. W. L. Thomas, Jr. Chicago: University of Chicago Press.

Mumford, L. 1961. *The city in history.* New York: Harcourt, Brace and World.

Naisbitt, J. 1982. *Mega trends.* New York: Warner Books.

Nakane, C. 1970. *Japanese society.* Berkeley: University of California Press.

Odum, H. W.; and Moore, H. 1938. *American regionalism: A cultural-historical approach to national integration.* New York: Henry Holt.

Outdoor Recreation Commission Caravan Surveys, Inc. 1968. "Visits of the United States Public to National Parks." USDI, National Park Service. Washington, D.C.

Parsons, T.; and Bales, R. F. 1955. *Family, socialization and interaction process.* Glencoe: The Free Press.

Pebley, A. R.; and Bloom, D. E. 1982. Childless Americans. *American Demographics* 4(1):18-21.

Phillip, S. F. 1976. Unpublished term paper. College Station, TX: Texas A & M University.

Planning Economics Group. 1981. Demographic forecast: Two income families. *American Demographics* 3(6):46-47.

Polsky, N. 1967. *Hustlers, beats and others.* Chicago: Aldine.

Potter, D. R.; Sharpe, K. M.; Hendee, J. C.; and Clark, R. N. 1972. *Questionnaires for research: An annotated bibliography on design, construction, and use.* USDA Forest Service Research Paper PNW-140. Portland, OR: Pacific Northwest Forest and Range Experiment Station.

Redl, F. 1966. *When we deal with children.* New York: The Free Press.

Reischauer, E. O. 1978. *The Japanese.* Cambridge: Harvard University Press.

Reiss, I. 1972. *The family system.* New York: Winterscourt Press.

Russell, C. 1981. Inside the shrinking household. *American Demographics* 3(9):28-33.

Sartre, J. 1957. *Being and nothingness.* Trans. H. Barnes. Secaucus, NJ: Citadel Press.

Sharpe, G. 1982. *Interpreting the environment,* 2nd ed. New York: John Wiley & Sons.

Smith, V. L., ed. 1977. *Hosts and guests: The anthropology of tourism.* Philadelphia: University of Pennsylvania Press.

Soldo, B. J. 1980. America's elderly in the 1980s. *Population Bulletin* (Nov.).

Stankey, G. H. 1973. *Visitor perception of wilderness recreation carrying capacity.* USDA Forest Service Research Paper INT-142. Ogden, UT: Intermountain Forest and Range Experiment Station.

Sussman, M. B.; and Burchinal, L. E. 1962. Kin family network: Unheralded structure in current conceptualization of family functioning. *Marriage and Family Living* 24:231-240.

Thomas, J. W.; and Dixon, R. A. 1974. Cemetery ecology. In *Symposium on wildlife in an urbanizing environment.* Planning and Resources Development Series #20. Amherst, MA: Cooperative Extension Service.

Tilden, F. (n.d.) *The fifth essence.* Washington: National Park Trust Board.

Tilden, F. 1977. *Interpreting our heritage.* Chapel Hill: University of North Carolina Press.

Travers, P. L. 1969. Only connect. In *Only connect: Readings on children's literature,* ed. S. Egoff, G. T. Stubbs, and L. F. Ashley, 132-206. New York: Oxford University Press.

Travers, R. M. W. 1967. *Research and theory related to audio-visual information transmission.* Washington, D.C.: U.S. Department of Health, Education and Welfare.

U.S. Department of Commerce. 1972. *A study of Japanese travel habits and patterns,* ed. K. Gess. Washington, DC: U.S. Travel Service, Office of Research and Analysis.

U.S. Department of Commerce. 1980. *1979 population estimates.* Washington, D.C.: Bureau of the Census.

U.S. Travel Service. 1978. *A regional analysis of international travel to the U.S.* Washington, D.C.: U.S. Department of Commerce.

Vogel, E. G. 1963. *Japan's new middle class.* Berkeley: University of California Press.

Wagar, J. A. 1972a. Evaluating interpretation and interpretive media. (Paper presented at the Association of Interpretive Naturalists Meeting, Callaway Gardens, Pine Mountain, Georgia, April 7, 1972).

Wagar, J. A. 1972b. *The recording quizboard: A device for evaluating interpretive services.* USDA Forest Service Research Paper PNW-139. Portland, OR: Pacific Northwest Forest and Range Experiment Station.

Warner, W. L. 1963. *Yankee city.* New Haven: Yale University Press.

Washburne, R. F. 1971. Visitor response to interpretive facilities at five visitor centers. Master's thesis, University of Washington, Seattle.

Washburne, R. F. and Wagar, J. A. 1972. Evaluating visitor response to exhibit content. *Curator* 15:248-254.

Webb, E. J.; Campbell, D. T.; Schwartz, R. D.; and Sechrest, L. 1966. *Unobtrusive measures: Nonreactive research in the social sciences.* Chicago: Rand McNally.

Weed, J. A. 1982. Divorce: American style. *American Demographics* 4(3):12-17.

Whyte, W. F. 1943. *Street corner society.* Chicago: University of Chicago Press.

Wicker, A. W. 1969. Attitudes versus actions: The relationship of verbal and overt behavioral responses to attitude objects. *Journal of Social Issues* 35(4):41-78.

Williams, J. D.; and Sofranko, A. J. 1980. *Rebirth of rural America: Rural migration in the midwest.* Ames, IA: North Central Regional Center for Development, Iowa State University.

Yankelovich, D. 1978. The new psychological contracts at work. *Psychology Today* (May).

Yankelovich, D. 1979. Work, values and the new breed. In *Work in America the decade ahead,* ed. C. Kerr and J. Rosow. New York: Van Nostrand Reinhold.

Yankelovich, D. 1981. *New rules: Searching for self-fulfillment in a world turned upside down.* New York: Random House.

Zaner, R. 1970. *The way of phenomenology.* New York: Pegasus.

Zelinsky, W. 1973. *The cultural geography of the United States.* Englewood Cliffs, NJ: Prentice-Hall.

INDEX